CHARITY MARIE

REFLECTIONS

A SHORT STORY

& NONFICTION COLLECTION

Reflections

Some names and identifying details of people described in this book have been altered to protect their privacy.

Hardback Edition

ISBN: 978-1-7378854-0-5

"Each story throughout REFLECTIONS is uniquely positive. The commonality throughout isn't just Charity's honesty about the good and bad which has inspired her world, but each piece shares a hopeful appreciation of life and the courageous choice it takes to live it."

—Jesse Friend

"One word summarizes this book…**wow!** I absolutely love it when authors take their time to paint the picture so vividly that you actually feel like you're in the room. That's what Charity does. She takes you there with her all the way with her details.

"Additionally, I felt the sincerity of her writing. She lets you in to her personal life through the reflections following the short story and I just love that final touch. I'm the type of person that sits back and watches the credits and behind the scenes of every film or show I watch to see what each scene meant to the writer because it makes me so much more emotionally invested.

"So, if you're anything like me, you will love this book! **Definitely a must read!"**

—Alisha Rose

"Have you ever read a book, thoroughly enjoyed it, and then wondered how the author came up with the story? Well, Reflections by Charity Marie is just like sitting down for coffee and a chat with your favorite author. **This book welcomes you in.**

"After each and every story, Charity opens up about how she got the idea for the characters, plot, etc. It's a rare opportunity to look inside an author's mind. The stories are all engaging, exciting, heart-warming, interesting, and are rich with details, both serious and frivolous. **I loved this book and think I'll grab a fresh cup of coffee and read it again!"**

—Lilli Ahmadpour

DEAR READER

I've been writing, at this point in my life, for more than 25 years. My career in writing has been long and varied, but it started when I was 14 years old. My 9th grade English teacher gave us a short story assignment. I wrote a piece called "Dark Walk" with a main character named Selena. It was a suspense/thriller story that I spent about a week writing. The assignment was for one page - I wrote 14. I received an A+ for the assignment, likely because of my enthusiasm and creativity rather than the true story merits. I loved the main character Selena so much, five years later I created a Star Wars role playing character for her. She was almost an alter-ego for me and she kicked butt in every way. She was powerful, strong, and fierce. I like to believe that as my first real character, she shaped me as much as I shaped her.

Since that time, I've dabbled in short stories and nonfiction every year, slowly but steadily adding to my collection. Some of the pieces have been published and some haven't. I'm very cognizant of the passing years, the whooshing of time as it passes. Now that I've effectively reached about the mid-point of my life, I feel a rush to accomplish all the things I set out to do.

In addition, writing is art, which is highly subjective. So, I'll let you, dear reader, be the judge of these stories. I have faith you'll enjoy reading them as much as I enjoyed writing them. The bond between author and reader is a special one that knows no boundaries. These stories are crafted with love, dedication, and as much skill as I possess. I hope you're able to savor them like a fine wine or meal.

Like most writers, my work is influenced by my life and experiences. It's amazing to me that even more than a decade after writing a story, I can remember exactly why I wrote it, where I was, and what inspired me. It's my hope these stories will resonate with you as much as they do with me. At the end of each piece, you'll find a short reflection on the work from my perspective as an author. This book is an intimate look at life through the lens of my writing.

Enjoy!

Charity Marie

ACKNOWLEDGMENTS

This book is for Robert, my dear, sweet husband. He is always the first to encourage me, has never once wavered in his absolute confidence in me, and is my best friend and soul mate for eternity.

Thank you, my love, for seeing this book before I ever could. Thank you for the gift of your love. I would be lost without it

PART ONE

Short Fiction

1 Blue

I sat in my wicker rocking chair, enjoying the cool fall morning, a welcome treat after the recent Texas heat. My current group of rescue dogs, eleven in total, chased each other, their excited barks ringing in the air. Watching them play always made me laugh. The shrill ringing of my cell phone broke through the noise. I tried not to groan. Bella, a pregnant dog at my feet, gazed at me and wagged her tail, thumping it against the wooden porch as I stood. The caller ID showed a local number. I moved inside, away from the noise.

"Hello, thank you for calling Man's Best Friend Rescue. This is Roxanne, how can I help you?"

"My name is Michelle. I have a dog to surrender. Do you have room?"

I hesitated. "Not really but maybe I can still help. We have a network of foster homes for dogs."

"His name is Blue. He's three years old and a Labrador mixed with a bird hunting dog, I forget the kind. We got him as a puppy. We thought it would be good practice. But then I got pregnant sooner than we expected. We just can't keep him anymore now that I'm about to have our second child."

I already had a feeling where this was going. "I see. How much does he weigh?"

"He's 90 pounds or so."

"Has he ever shown signs of aggression?"

There was a long pause. "If I say yes, will you still take him? All the other rescues have turned me down. If you don't take him, I'll have to take him to the pound, where they'll just kill him. I don't want that."

As I suspected. Now, we were getting somewhere. "I'm a certified dog behaviorist, trained to rehabilitate dogs. Many rescues can't handle problematic animals. Why don't you tell me real quick what happened?"

The words tumbled forth. "It wasn't Blue's fault. My son Nathan is almost three. He's a handful. I think Blue was just trying to get my son to leave him alone. I've told him a hundred times not to pull on Blue's ears. Anyway, I turned away for a second. Next thing I knew Nathan was screaming with blood pouring out of his arm. He needed six stitches on his forearm. The doctor told me we should euthanize Blue. Once a dog bites a human, it will again." She took a deep breath. "I'm sure Blue never meant to hurt him. It was an accident. He's a good dog."

"Okay, let me ask you, did Blue growl first? Were there signs of stress before he bit?"

"Well, not then. We've had some close calls before where Blue snapped at Nathan but never actually bit him. I was always right there to stop it."

I nodded. "Could you give me your address? I'll swing by this afternoon to meet Blue. If he passes a couple simple tests, I can try to find him another home."

"Oh, God," she started crying into the phone. "Thank you. You're such a lifesaver. I didn't know what I was going to do. He's got the sweetest personality and most beautiful eyes. You'll see."

After a quick lunch, I checked on the dogs to make sure they had plenty of water. Then I loaded up my beat-up Ford F-150 with my largest crate, a leash, and some treats. Michelle's house, a squat ranch style brick, was close to the center of the small town of Barlett. A chain link fence surrounded it and toys scattered the yard. A young boy watched me walk up. A white bandage coated in mud wrapped his arm. A yellow dump truck sat half full of black wet mud beside him, and a growing pile of mud several inches tall.

"Hi, are you Nathan?" I asked. He didn't respond. I frowned. "Is your mommy home?"

The boy looked back at the truck and started adding more dirt to it. When he didn't respond, I opened the gate and closed it behind me. "What are you making there?" I asked.

Nathan stared. Something about his stare made me pause. I knelt before him. His gaze darted away to skitter around the yard.

"Hi, I'm Roxanne. Are you Nathan?"

His gaze slid away and then he slapped the mud beside him, hard, sending it flying. I flinched as a big glob landed on my cheek and in my hair.

The screen door opened. A blonde-haired young woman wearing jeans and a bright red t-shirt popped her head around the door frame. "Nathan, time for your nap. Oh, you must be Roxanne! I didn't realize you were here. Come on inside."

I rose, wiping mud off my cheek. Michelle hesitated then opened the door wider. She looked from Nathan to me and understanding dawned in her eyes. She released the door, which slammed shut, as she trotted barefoot down the steps. "What happened? Did Nathan do that?"

"It's okay. A 150-pound wet dog will do much worse." I said chuckling. I bent to the side, running a hand through my short red hair. A big clump of mud fell to the ground.

"Oh, I'm so sorry. Nathan's autistic and nonverbal." Michelle reached for her son's hand. In a firm tone she said, "Sweetie, it's time to go inside." A piercing scream tore through the air and I jumped. I backed away, horrified as Nathan began kicking at his mother's legs. She stepped aside but not before several blows struck her shins. Michelle said, her voice tight and controlled. "Nathan, no kicking! Timeout."

The scream continued, a never-ending caterwaul that rang in all directions. I stepped further away, unsure what I should do. When Nathan took a breath, Michelle spoke again. "I need just a minute to calm him down. I'll come outside with Blue." She scooped him up in her arms, put his legs around her hip. They proceeded inside, with Nathan slapping her and screaming the whole way.

I sighed and clasped my hands together to stop their shaking. Adrenaline rushed through my body, setting my nerves on edge. A few houses away, a woman stood on her porch, watching, with her arms crossed. Nathan's periodic screams broke the silence of the neighborhood. Moments later, Michelle returned, pulling Blue by the collar, and released him out the door. He was lean, long-legged, with a golden short-haired coat broken up by a big patch of white on his chest, belly, and paws. A small smudge of white, looking like a misplaced glob of paint, dotted his large head. His muzzle was a creamy mix of pink, white, and gold.

Another scream filled the air. Blue's tail dropped between his legs, his head fell lower and he shivered on the front step. "Move, Blue!" Michelle gave him a nudge in the rear with her knee. Blue jumped down the steps, startled. I watched as he moved aside, and Michelle came back toward me. With every shriek, Blue flinched and his body language grew more skittish.

"Here boy," I called, holding out my hand. Blue's eyes, a soft cerulean blue with inky black irises looked at me with an expression of sadness so deep my stomach clenched. He took a tentative step, then froze as another scream burst out the front door.

"I'm sorry, I'll be right back," Michelle said, sprinting back into the house. I tried to ignore the woman's screams over her son's.

I knelt, pulling a treat out of my pocket. "Blue, come," I said in a gentle tone and held it out. He stepped toward me, slow and cautious, tail still tucked between his legs, ears flat against his head. "It's okay, boy. Good boy, keep coming." The pieces of the puzzle started to come together, the answers shimmering in his eyes as he begged me for forgiveness. His hindquarters dropped lower with every step until he was almost crawling.

Still screams continued to burst from the house. Blue halted a few feet away, unable to come any further. "Hey pretty boy, it's okay, I'll come to you" I murmured, taking a couple slow steps toward him. Blue laid flat on the ground, head between his paws in a position of utter submission as clear as I'd ever seen in an animal. "Oh, you poor baby. You just don't understand any of this, do you? It's not your fault, sweetheart." I held a treat in front of his nose. His tongue reached forward to lick at my fingers. I laid it down and he scooped it up with his tongue. He crunched the treat and looked at me, then flopped over on his side, exposing his belly for me to scratch. I rubbed him and sat next to him, with my legs crisscrossed. I took several deep breaths as my hands continued to shake.

I looked toward the house, sudden silence now making me nervous. Blue rolled over, then crawled forward, putting one timid paw on my leg. His head was almost level with mine. He crept forward until he was in my lap, cuddled against me like a small child. He shivered and licked my hand.

Michelle returned, closing the door behind her without making a sound. She came to stand before me. Exhaustion and embarrassment came off her in waves. "I'm so very sorry about all that."

Up close, Michelle appeared around seven months pregnant. She stood above me with her hands on her hips, chest heaving, and face flushed. "I would invite you inside but—"

"Oh no need, we're good out here." I made my decision in an instant. "With your permission, I'd like to take him."

"Seriously? Just like that?" she asked, her brown eyes wide. "I thought you needed to test him or something?"

I smiled at her. "I already did. He passed with flying colors. In fact, I think he'll make an ideal emotional support animal. I work with a military veteran's group. He'll be perfect with some training."

Tears overflowed Michelle's eyes as she knelt next to me. Blue looked at her. She rested her head on his, sobbing while he licked her face. She lifted her tear-streaked face, "Are you sure? You'll take care of him?"

I smiled and nodded. "Absolutely. With some time, training, and other dogs, Blue'll be just fine. He'll have a chance to redeem himself."

"Could I see him sometime? You know, see how he's doing?"

I knew she wouldn't, but I spoke with complete honesty. "Whenever you like."

She wiped away her tears. "I've got some money inside, could I donate? It's not much, just fifty dollars. Oh, you'll need his shot records and things. You can have it all. Let me get them for you."

With a gentle nudge, I pushed Blue from my lap and stood, clipping a leash to his collar. "That would be wonderful." Without even a tug, he followed me out of the gate and jumped onto the seat of my truck as if he belonged there all along.

Author Reflections

I wrote this story as an homage to a dog named Blue who briefly came into our lives. Unfortunately, he bit my daughter twice without provocation, so we had to return him to the shelter, but not before he sparked this story in my heart. We suspect something in his history made him more aggressive than he should have been, and it was beyond my ability to address.

This story is what I wish I had been able to do for him. Since then, we've adopted Rory, who has become a service dog for us and is as sweet and loyal as a dog can be. She joins our other service dog, Max, who is nine and starting to slow down due to age. I regularly hope that Blue found a safe home and regret that it wasn't with us.

Other elements of this story are based on things I know happen every day around the country. The little boy in the story is somewhat loosely based on my son, Phoenix, who has autism and struggled a great deal when he was younger. I tried to be realistic about the portrayal of autism but in a sympathetic way. Anyone with autism or who has experience with it, knows autism manifests differently from person to person. The boy in the story is not meant to be representative of all people with autism, just an example of it. No two people will have the same struggles and challenges.

We are blessed that our son, now a teenager, has outgrown many autistic traits. It's thanks to a great deal of factors including love, patience, plus help from therapists over many years. He used to scream at loud sounds endlessly so sirens, fire alarms, even bells at school would cause a fit of screaming and crying. He has since outgrown that, thankfully. He has turned into a six foot plus giant of an almost man, who is one of the sweetest, gentlest souls you could ever hope to meet. I will always remember him as a sweet, vulnerable, sensitive red-haired seven-year-old in need of my love and protection, no matter how big he gets.

2
Deuces

Jessie wiped her hands on her jeans before picking up her cards. She tried to ignore the camera looming in front of her. The crowd around the final table at the World Series of Poker event kept quiet while she used the time to decide. Across from her were two other players, both men, both far more experienced.

In the center of the table were three cards: a jack of spades, a ten of spades and a two of hearts. Jessie looked at her hand again. Still a pair of queens, one a heart, and the other a spade. The bet was one hundred thousand chips. Her chips were a little over five million, so it wasn't that she couldn't play the hand. Someone else had made the bet, which likely meant much bigger face cards than hers. Likely kings or aces.

"You fallin' asleep on us there, little lady?" the man to her right said, chuckling. He leaned back in his seat and adjusted his big cowboy hat before picking up his whiskey to sip.

The other man stayed silent, not making eye contact. Bravado from the cowboy, and avoidance from the other player. One of them was overconfident, and the other one either had a bigger hand or trips. Jessie decided to find out.

"I raise," she said and paused as the crowd gasped in unison. She leaned forward, counted out her chips, then said, "Five hundred thousand." She set them in front of her within reach of the dealer. The cowboy sat forward, squinting at her.

"You sure you wanna do that? Pretty bold move, I'd say."

Jessie smiled. "I guess that makes me a pretty bold woman then."

The cowboy looked at the man across from him. "Well, T-Rex, what're you gonna do, son?"

T-Rex didn't speak, simply pushed his chips in toward the dealer, the universal sign of a call.

"I call," the cowboy said and pushed his chips forward. Betting completed, the dealer discarded a card and flipped over the next. An ace of spades showed. Jessie's heart sank. The spade gave her a chance at a flush but would give pocket aces three of a kind. She looked to the cowboy.

"You probably know what I'm gonna do next, if you're any kind of player. I'm all in," he said. He was betting out of turn, a clear sign he had at least a pair of aces. Jessie estimated his chips and realized they were evenly matched. Her call of his bet would leave her with about fifty thousand chips.

T-Rex folded without a word.

"I call," Jessie said and flipped up her hand. The cowboy showed a pair of aces, giving him three of a kind, then sat back with a satisfied smirk.

"You're outgunned, ma'am."

Jessie cocked her head and smiled. "Am I? Pretty sure I can draw to any king and any spade. Gives me lots of outs."

"You're taking a helluva chance betting all your chips on a draw. Rookie play," he replied.

"We'll see."

The tension in the room made the hair on the back of Jessie's hair stand on end. She could feel sweat trickling down her sides. Her legs trembled beneath her. Her gut screamed at her this was the right play. It defied any kind of poker logic but somehow, she knew the next card would be a king.

The dealer discarded a card and flipped up the next one. It was a king of spades.

"It's a royal flush, the best possible hand!" the announcer bellowed as the crowd roared with delight. Jessie couldn't believe her eyes. She looked at the cowboy, who stared stunned at the card. His face grew red. A nearby staff member put their hand on his shoulder to guide him away from the table. He shrugged the man off and grabbed his drink. The dealer pushed the pile of chips in front of her.

"You got lucky. Even a dog has its day."

From around her, there were boos and hisses at his words. A security guard joined the staff member and guided him away. Over his shoulder he said, "You ever come up against me again, you won't stand a chance! I promise you that!"

Jessie sat back, trying to control her breathing. Her heart was racing in her chest, and she was almost giddy. Her chip stack had doubled, and she set to work organizing it for betting.

"Well played," T-Rex said. "I had pocket tens."

Jessie paused. She'd bet him out of the pot with trip-tens? But it had been the right play. He wasn't in a good position to play the hand, especially with bigger hands possible.

The dealer shuffled and dealt the next hand. For the next hour they sparred back and forth, neither one having a good enough hand to make a daring play. Then Jessie looked down to see pocket twos. She suppressed a groan.

Deuces were one of the hardest hands to play. Without either another two or the cards for a straight or a full house, they were useless. Bored and tired of the back and forth, she called and watched the dealer flip the cards. A five of hearts, a king of diamonds, and a ten of clubs. A complete mish-mash but a pair up with any of those cards meant certain defeat for her hand. There was no guarantee he had a pair at all. He checked, passing the bet to her. She checked as well. The next card was an ace of spades and Jessie suppressed a smile. It felt almost like an omen.

"Bet one million chips," T-Rex said. Jessie hesitated for a moment, thinking hard. Had he set a trap? Did he have an ace? Most players would have raised on such a hand playing head-to-head but his chip stack was much less than hers. After all the back and forth, had he studied her and learned enough about to predict her actions? Was he bluffing or serious?

In an instant, she decided to trust her gut for the second time that day. She called. The dealer showed the next card: a two of diamonds. Jessie tried not to react, told herself to act natural. She slumped ever so slightly in her seat, then looked to T-Rex for his bet.

"I'm all in," he proclaimed, making eye contact with her.

What could he have to be that confident? Then she realized. He had two pair. King-ten would be a powerful hand at this point of the game. And with a two on the board, he would believe he couldn't be beat. No way someone would hold on to pocket twos until this point.

"I call," Jessie said. She held the cards in her hand and looked at T-Rex, who was studying her, his eyes intense. He turned his cards over, showing a king and a ten. She turned hers up. His eyes widened in disbelief.

"Trip-twos. We have a new World Series of Poker winner for 2019! Jessie Aranyo is this year's world champion and the first woman to ever win the World Series of Poker main event!"

Jessie felt the air leave her lungs for a long moment. The crowd erupted in roars, whistles, clapping, and cheers. T-Rex looked too stunned to move.

Jessie got up and walked around the table. She held out her hand for him to shake. "Congratulations. You're a millionaire. That was an excellent game."

T-Rex stood, towering over her, and looked down at Jessie. "It was an excellent game. You know what this means right?"

Jessie shook her head.

"It means first place buys breakfast."

Jessie laughed, all the tension and adrenaline flowing out with it. "You're got a deal" Together they turned to face the camera and the dealer to cash out

Author Reflections

I love this story. At only 1,300 words, it's pretty short but every time I read it, the story gets my adrenaline going. That's always been the reader feedback as well. I wrote this story to be an homage to poker, a game I love dearly. Unfortunately, there aren't a lot of places interested in publishing a flash fiction poker story, no matter how good it is. I've been playing poker only slightly longer than I've been writing. I started at age 8 playing poker at the parties my father would host at home. It was penny poker, but I was good at it. I made $25 one night and after that they wouldn't play with my any more. I remember my uncle Scott telling me I was a natural at cards. I didn't know what he meant at the time. I just knew I loved the game. Now, years later, I'm a professional player who regularly plays both cash and tournaments. It's not something I will ever do full time but I enjoy playing 2-4 times a week. One of my favorite places to play in Texas is Rounders in San Antonio. If you're in the area, check it out and say hi if I'm there.

Jessie's story combines a lot of elements I encounter in poker all the time. As a male dominated game, it's not unusual at all for the men around me to not only underestimate my skill level, but to simply believe, despite all evidence to the contrary, that I can't play. A lot of the time, it's unintentional. For all the disbelief I receive, I also receive an enormous amount of respect as well. I tried to reflect the respect in T-Rex and the disbelief in the cowboy (who is deliberately unnamed).

Poker players will hopefully enjoy this short story at one of the world's premiere poker games Hopefully, those who aren't familiar with the game might develop an interest in it. It's definitely a dream of mine to play in and place at a World Series of Poker event. I've learned poker has made me a better person - better at analysis, better at judging people and their character, and a stronger negotiator in business. It's given me more confidence to promote my work. Because on the poker felt, all that matters are the cards, the players and what you do with both. I've learned, it's the same with life.

3 Lost Heritage

It had been a great, beautiful city once, long ago. For some reason, the desolation affected me and made my stomach clench into a hard knot of sorrow. I could picture the grand promenade as it had looked with handsome couples strolling hand in hand as they laughed and talked on their way to dinner. The theater house sat on a hill at the end of the lane as if looking down to view its soon-to-be-patrons. The concrete was crumbling to dust, and several pillars lay against their brother for support. Other pillars weren't so lucky, and their remains were scattered, with broken, chipped, and ragged edges. I moved with great care, stepping over and around crumbling pieces, trying not to disturb anything. The wind blew in a heavy sigh full of grit, forcing me to shield my eyes and nose for a moment as it swept past.

"Julie, are you okay?" Rob's hand touched my elbow and I jumped, a mixture of surprise and the strange electricity that sparked in me any time Rob got too close.

"Yes, of course. Sorry, I was just thinking." I replied, hoping he wouldn't notice the slight tremble in my voice. My emotions were raw today. Being here was hard, harder than I had thought it would be. I was desperate to find them, even after so many years of searching.

"Care to share with the rest of the class?"

I chuckled at the old joke and then looked back out at the landscape. I knew the city's story almost as well as I knew my own. Over a hundred years ago, a great tsunami had swept through the city, caused by one of the worst earthquakes ever recorded. It had happened so fast that the only survivors were those who were fortunate enough to be out of the area for whatever reason. A series of sandstorms had followed, further partially burying the remains.

Rob looked out at the crumbled city. "It's hard to believe, huh?"

I nodded, unable to think of a better reply.

Prior to the devastation, the city had survived years of conflict including hostile conquest by the Roman Empire hundreds of years before. Nothing created by humans could prevent the devastation that came from the sea.

Rob spoke again. "Did I hear you tell Steve last night some of your family lived in this city?"

"Yes, my great grandfather and his son were still in the city when the tsunami hit. My great grandmother was out of the country visiting our relatives in the U.S. with her daughter, my grandmother. They had no warning." I closed my eyes for a moment to let the images wash over me. I tried to picture my great grandfather playing catch with his son or watching the sunset. I tried to picture anything other than the image of a huge wave crushing the city beneath it.

The walkie-talkie on my hip gave a shrill burst of feedback and then a crackling noise before a voice came booming from it. "Julie, it's Josh. Do you read me? Over."

I pulled the talkie from its clip and pressed the button. "Yes, I read you. Over."

"We found something in the northwest quadrant you need to see." The excitement in his voice was unmistakable. I broke into a jog, Rob right behind me.

When we arrived, there was tense excitement lingering in the air like a scent. We stood before a single-story house. Much of the roof was missing, and the support columns were eaten away by weather, bugs, and time. The door and windows were gaping holes and sagging wood. I paused, eyeing the ground leading to the door. A path had been taped off, just wide enough for people and equipment to pass. I pulled a pair of latex gloves from my back pocket, my fingers trembling. From a box by the doorway, I retrieved a pair of disposable booties and slipped them over my shoes. Rob copied my movements. Neither of us spoke as we stepped through the doorway into the foyer.

"Josh, where are you?" I yelled into the house.

"Here!" His voice came to us from the left, so I followed the hallway in that direction, peering in the various rooms until we came to the one at the end of the hallway. Inside, a path had been cleared of debris. I followed it to another smaller room, the remnants of a bathroom. Inside three members of my team huddled together, talking in hushed tones.

"What've you got?" I asked.

Josh turned to face me along with the other men, allowing me to see beyond them. In the tub were the skeletons of two humans, one larger and one smaller. In a moment, I could tell both were males from their pelvic bones. My mind made the leap before I could stop it. I looked at Josh, stunned.

"Is it? Could it be?"

Josh grinned at me. "I think it absolutely could. We won't know without DNA testing. They seem to be almost perfectly preserved, considering the amount of time. A section of the room collapsed creating an airlock of sorts. Check this out." He pushed past us and back into the bedroom. Emily worked in a far corner of the room, dusting and clearing in a widening circle atop of a half-collapsed wide chest of drawers covered with a variety of objects. Josh picked up something from a nearby cleared table and held it out to me.

"See anyone you know?"

I cradled it in my hands, cupping the picture frame by its edges. Looking back at me was a woman, a man, and two young children, a boy and a girl. One face was as familiar to me as my own. I felt the urge to sit and my legs began to give out. Rob caught my arm and gripped me around the waist to steady me.

"Okay, Jules?"

I glanced at him, noting the concern on his face, and nodded, happy for his support, nonetheless. He didn't pull away as I stared down at the photo again. My voice didn't sound like my own when I spoke. "It's them."

The room filled with whoops and cheers as my team celebrated our victory. I heard high fives behind me as I sank to my knees. The photo was hardly damaged and had only yellowed a little around the edges.

"Looks like the photo frame did a good job protecting the photo," Rob said.

Tears filled my eyes. I couldn't stop the rush of emotions pouring out of my gut, meeting up with my heart and filling every core of my being. A small sob broke free and the room fell silent around me. Someone's hand came to rest on my shoulder, and I looked up at Josh as a tear dripped off my chin.

"You did it, Jules. Now you can bring your family home." I collapsed against Rob and let my emotions go. Josh ushered everyone out of the room as Rob held me and let me cry.

"I can't believe it. Am I dreaming? "

Rob shook his head and I turned to look at him. "I've been trying to find them for so many years. So many times, I thought I had."

Rob smiled. "I guess perseverance wins the day again, huh?" He brushed a loose strand of hair behind my ear. I realized how close we were. His eyes were a brilliant green as he looked straight into mine. All I saw was kindness, acceptance, and understanding. I leaned forward and brushed his lips with mine. In it, I put my gratitude, friendship, happiness, and sorrow. He responded by submitting to my kiss and deepening it. At that moment, I realized what it meant to find your home. He pulled back, and left longing, and a sharp pang for more.

"I'm sorry, I probably shouldn't have done that." I felt the heat in my cheeks.

"Why? I've wanted to do that for ages." He replied. I looked at him, stunned to see him grinning. I couldn't help but smile, which turned into a laugh.

"Ages? Really? You're making archeology jokes, now?"

He laughed. "I've had my eye on you for quite a while. It's about time you noticed."

I laughed again, feeling relief and a new mixture of feelings blossom within my core. It mixed with the grief and pain and somehow made it okay. I looked at the photo again and smiled. I realized even amongst death and decay, there can be life, beauty, and hope.

Rob stood and helped me to my feet. "You, okay?"

I beamed at him. "I'm great, I think. I do have a phone call to make. My family needs to hear about this as soon as possible."

"I'll drive you." He led the way out of the room.

In the doorway, I turned back to look. A small sunbeam had managed to make its way in through the broken window. A swirl of dust hung in the air but somehow, the light made the area feel alive somehow. Finally, the rest of my family was found.

Author Reflections

This is one of those stories that was simply inspired. Unlike the last two stories, this one came to me from the ether, if you will. I am a member of a writing community called Writing.com and have been for more than a decade at this point. There was a contest with a picture prompt and in a millisecond, this story was born. It would go on to win first place in the site-wide contest.

I particularly love it for the optimistic, hopeful ending full of the promise of a bright future ahead for Julie. It felt to me like a great burden had been lifted from her and she was free to fully embrace life. Sometimes in life, things shackle us to old ways of thinking or behaving and it isn't until we're free of those things, we truly begin to live. I recently experienced that in real life, and it was the most joyful, freeing thing I've ever experienced in my life. I would encourage you to look for what's holding you back from your full potential and unchain yourself from it. Find your new beginning — it's never too late.

4 The Heist

Elise Forester opened the door and a cheery chime filled the air. Wall-to-wall clear glass cases full of sparkling jewelry jammed the store's interior. A slender older man with silver hair, dressed in a dapper black suit approached and held out his hand. "You must be the detective."

Elise shook the proffered hand, trying not to cringe at the man's clammy grip. "That's right. I understand there's a ring missing?"

"Yes, I'm the owner, Jim Tosh. One of our sales staff met with a gentleman who asked to see our engagement rings. Sabine, can you come here please?"

A slim, dark haired young woman emerged from a back room. Her eyes were rimmed in red and her porcelain skin flushed. She held a wadded-up tissue in one hand.

"Can you tell me what happened?" Elise asked, pulling out a pen and a small notepad from her back pocket.

Sabine took a deep breath, sniffled hard, and began in halting, broken sentences. "He looked normal. He came in like everyone does. He walked the room. Asked to see our one carat and larger rings. We talked about budget. He didn't really tell me about the woman he was buying the ring for which now seems strange."

"What was his budget?"

"That was the other strange part - he said he didn't have one, it was more about the quality of the ring."

"Did he look like he could afford it?"

Sabine stopped and looked to the right. "I think so. He wore a nice suit. Expensive shoes. Gold cuff links. He flirted with me a little bit."

"Do men do that often when shopping for engagement rings?" Sabine cocked her head, her piercing green eyes staring into Elise's. "Sometimes." Elise studied the woman. She was attractive, if a little waif-thin. "What happened next? What rings did he see?"

"I showed him five rings, ranging from one carat to five carats."

"Which one's missing?"

"The five-carat ring. It was almost perfect, nearly flawless."

"What's the value?"

Jim spoke up. "It's our most expensive ring. $150,000."

"Is it insured?"

Jim nodded. "They all are."

Elise looked around the store and then toward the back room. "Anyone else around in the store? Did you turn your back for a moment? Maybe walk away to get another ring?"

Sabine shook her head and Jim spoke. "Our policy is if someone needs to step away for something, we call another team member over to assist. The client is never unsupervised with jewelry."

"What about surveillance?"

Jim pointed to the ceiling. "A full HD system."

"Let's see the video."

They left Sabine and went into the back room to a computer monitor. Jim navigated the menus to bring up the video. Multiple views showed different angles in the store. Jim rewound the video.

"I'll need a copy of this."

Jim nodded. "I've already reviewed it, didn't see anything strange. I made a copy as well."

"Was there ever a time when the rings weren't visible?"

Jim looked at Elise. "Yes, actually, when Sabine puts the tray back, her head blocked the camera."

"How long has Sabine worked here? How was her background check?"

"Almost a year. Passed a background check and drug screening."

"Ever have any issues with her?"

Jim shook his head. "She's a model employee."

"What's her pay rate?"

"$10 an hour plus commission."

"Does she sell well?"

"Not as good as some of my staff but she does okay."

"Any money troubles you know of?" Did her boyfriend ever come to visit her during lunch?"

"I don't really know anything about her personal life."

"Have you ever seen the gentleman before?"

"Not that I recall."

"Did he seem familiar at all? Could he be a former employee?"

Jim shook his head.

"Let's see the video." Jim pressed play and Elise sat in the chair in front of the screen, watching closely. After a few moments, she straightened.

"Where has Sabine been since that time?"

"She went to the break room and the bathroom."

"Did she leave the store at any point after the man left?"

"She went to grab some lunch at Subway in Walmart right after she finished with him. She brought back a sandwich. Now that I think of it, it was a bit early for lunch, around 11."

Elise almost laughed. "That's perfect. Walmart has tons of cameras."

Jim looked confused. "Why does that matter?"

"I have a hunch Sabine did more than get lunch."

"I don't understand," Jim said.

"I'll be right back." A few minutes later her hunch was confirmed. On the Walmart surveillance system Sabine and the gentleman from the store met, she pulled something small from her pocket and handed it to him. He examined it, the overhead lights sparkling brightly off the stone. Elise collected a copy of the video and returned to the store.

Jim greeted Elise at the door. Sabine stood a short distance away, eyes downcast. Elise walked over to her. "Tell me again about the man who came into the store." Sabine's eyes flew to meet Elise's.

"What do you mean?"

"How do you know him?"

Sabine swallowed. "I don't know him."

"Is he a boyfriend?"

Sabine shook her head, her eyes wide.

"Your brother?"

She shook her head again. "I've never seen him before in my life."

"Then why did you have lunch with him and give him the ring?"

Sabine gasped. "I didn't."

Elise smiled. "Actually, you did. I have video of you and him getting very cozy at the Subway down the street."

Sabine's mouth dropped open and she stepped backward. A pulse raced at the side of her neck and her eyes darted around the store.

The smile vanished from Elise's face. "You have the right to remain silent. Anything you say can and will be used against you in a court of law. You have the right to an attorney..." Elise pulled handcuffs off her belt and grasped Sabine's arm.

"Wait," she gasped, pulling on her arm. "Please, wait. I didn't have a choice."

Elise paused for a moment. "Explain."

Tears spilled from Sabine's eyes. "I will if you promise not to arrest me. I can't go to jail."

"Depends on what you have to say. Start talking."

"Please, you've got to help me. He said he'd kill my daughter if I didn't do it."

Jim stepped forward. "You have a child? You never mentioned her."

"I didn't want you to not give me overtime. She stays with my sister while I'm at work."

Elise let go of Sabine's arm. "Start from the beginning."

The words tumbled over each other in a rush. "Two weeks ago, he followed me home from the store. He grabbed me at my door, pushed me inside, and told me I had to steal the most expensive ring in the store and give it to him. He showed me a picture of Sasha and told me he'd kill her. He said the rings were insured, if we did it right, no one would ever find out. He told me exactly how to do it, how to avoid the camera being able to see the empty place on the tray."

"Did he tell you his name?"

Sabine shook her head.

"Where's Sasha now?"

"She's at her preschool until 3."

"You need to call your sister, have her take your daughter home."

Sabine looked at the floor then at her boss. "Mr. Tosh, I'm so sorry."

Elise looked over at the store owner. "You can guarantee he'll be back. Crooks like him are always greedy."

Sabine nodded. "That's what he said when I met with him. He said he'd be in touch."

"When?"

"Tonight, after work. He's going to meet me at the house."

"Do you have a phone number for him?"

"There's a number he sends me texts from." She pulled a phone from her pocket and showed Elise.

Elise jotted it down. "We'll trace the call and pick him up. It's unlikely we'll be able to recover the ring. For now, Sabine, I need to take you in for a statement, but I won't handcuff you if you cooperate. Okay?"

Sabine nodded. Elise put her hand on Sabine's upper arm and escorted her to the car outside. Once Sabine was in the car, Elise looked down the street. At the corner, a tall man in a jogging suit watched them. Elise's eyes met his for only a moment before he walked in the opposite direction, dropping a small black flip phone in a nearby trash can.

Elise took off running. She rounded the corner, hand on her gun, but the street was empty. She took a few steps forward, looking for any sign of him but he was gone. She ran down the narrow street to the next corner and looked both directions. Looking to the right she spotted the man walking through a small crowd. She followed him for a few blocks undetected. It was a diner window that gave her away on the other side of the street. She knew the moment he recognized her because he took off running through a crosswalk. She raced after him, dodging people who jumped or shouted their surprise.

"Stop, police!" Elise yelled as loud as she could. The man continued to run full speed ahead. He turned toward a nearby overpass and ran to the middle of it. Elise followed him and stopped as he climbed up on the ledge above the highway. Time seemed to slow.

Elise's breaths came fast. "Sir… please… let's talk for a moment."

"Talk? About what? You're just a cop, what do you care?"

"I care because I'm a cop. Let's talk about why you want to jump off an overpass."

"That's my business. You just stay there."

Elise raised her hands but inched forward when he turned to look at the highway below. The rushing sound of vehicles filled the air and made the overpass vibrate.

"Listen, we can work this out. You don't need to do this."

The man shook his head and looked at her, grinning. "Yes, I do. I'm not going to jail."

"Who said anything about jail? I just wanted to ask you a couple questions. You know, about the phone you threw away."

The man laughed and returned to watching the cars pass. Elise moved forward a couple steps. "Hey, I said stay there!"

Elise froze, now less than three feet away. Could she grab him if he jumped? The jogging suit didn't look sturdy enough to not rip if she grabbed it so it would have to be an arm. Though the man was trim and fit, he outweighed her by at least seventy-five pounds and was six inches taller.

"Please, don't do this. Let me help you."

The man smiled back at her over his shoulder, faced forward, and jumped. For a moment Elise froze in disbelief, then she raced to the ledge and watched as the man fell through the air. Vehicles below passed, some swerving as their astonished owners watched in disbelief. The man missed catching the back of a tractor trailer by six inches, landing on the pavement. His legs crumpled beneath him, and she watched him writhing on the ground, a growing pool of blood on the ground. She looked around for a way down and found a steep decline to the road. She ran for it and rounded the corner to see the man on his feet, limping badly. A semi swerved, narrowly missing him and almost clipping the back of another car. The sound of squealing tires and air brakes filled the air. Horns soon joined the cacophony of sounds as Elise waited for an opening to cross the road.

He made it to the slow lane, his leg dragging uselessly behind him. Elise could see a fuel tanker with a bright yellow LOVES logo on the side heading for him. The driver's head was down, a phone in his hand.

"Look out," Elise yelled at the top of her lungs. The man turned to look but in a blink it was over. The semi brakes squealed a full second after the impact, causing the tanker to jackknife sideways and into a guardrail. All around vehicles swerved to avoid each other. After a few minutes of panicked drivers, people slowed, rubbernecking the accident. The man's body lay crumpled and bloody in front of the tractor trailer.

"It's going to be such a long day," Elise murmured to herself and radioed dispatch for assistance. She checked on the truck driver, who was shaken, clearly in shock, and babbling nonsense in a thick Spanish accent that increased when he saw the body.

She guided him a safe distance away to sit on the side of the road, after determining where his emergency gear was. She put out flares and hazard signs, then began guiding traffic away from the area in the other two lanes. Traffic rapidly began to back up. After about ten minutes, several patrol cars, two firetrucks, and a pair of ambulances arrived.

She left the traffic guidance to a patrol officer and returned to the scene. She grabbed a pair of gloves from the EMT and then stared at the body for a moment. "Damn, I wish you had let me arrest you." She probed the man's pockets. All were empty of ID. Not even any keys. Elise sighed. "It was a long shot anyway."

Elise walked up to the officer in charge, explained what had happened, and then headed back to the jewelry store. She looked at her watch. It had been over an hour since she escorted Sabine to her patrol car. Elise found Sabine sitting inside the store on a stool while Jim helped a customer. Elise gestured toward the back room.

"What happened?" Sabine demanded. "Why did you leave?"

"The man who threatened you was watching the store. I saw him watching us at the street corner and pursued him. He won't be bothering you or Sasha again."

"You caught him?" she asked.

Elise shook her head and looked at the ground for a moment before taking a deep breath. "Not exactly."

"You didn't arrest him? Why not?"

Jim Tosh entered the room. "Detective Forester, what happened?"

"I was just telling Sabine I followed the thief. Unfortunately, he was hit by a semi and didn't survive the encounter."

Jim's eyebrows rose. "Oh, dear. Are you sure it was him?"

"I'm afraid so. It's the man from the video."

Sabine sat in a nearby chair, breathing hard. "It's over? You mean, it's really over?"

Elise nodded. Sabine burst into tears, rocking in the chair, arms clutched around her stomach.

Elise and Jim stood and tried not to watch, unsure what to do. Elise cleared her throat. "I was able to recover the phone he threw in the trash. Hopefully there are fingerprints that will lead us to an address. He may not have had an opportunity to contact a fence yet to sell the ring. I will find it if I can and return it to you."

Jim held out his hand and Elise shook it. "Thank you, Detective, for all you did today."

Sabine stood, walked over, and without a word, hugged Elise. Her arms trembled from the fierceness of the embrace. Her words came, choked with emotion. "Thank you so much. Thank you for saving my daughter."

Elise patted the girl's back. "I'm still going to need that statement."

Sabine wiped the tears from her face. "Of course. Anything I can do to help." Sabine looked at Jim. "I will gather my things. I'm so sorry about all of this."

Jim held out a hand to Sabine. She took it and he covered her hand with his other one. "You are a victim in all of this. You did what any mother would do. I wish you had come to me so I could help you, but I understand why you did what you did. I expect you to take a couple days off, with pay, and enjoy some time with your daughter. Then I'll see you here bright and early Saturday morning."

Tears fell once more from Sabine's green eyes. "Oh, Mr. Tosh, thank you so much. You are such a wonderful man." She wrapped her arms around him in a hug. He smiled at Elise and winked. Together, Sabine and Elise returned to Elise's car and headed for the police department.

Author Reflections

This is another story that came about through a prompt and won a Writing.com contest. I then expanded the story. I've always had a love of true crime and mysteries, so I used that knowledge to create a fun jewelry heist mystery short story. I enjoyed working on this little caper. For anyone who is a writer, know that this final draft of the story was after at least a dozen revisions, and the ending came after a great deal of struggle. Sometimes a story takes a while to find its own way.

I particularly love Sabine's character - her desperation and fear as a mother felt very real for me when I was writing the story as was her relief. Elise, the competent, fierce female detective spoke to me too. I love how she fearlessly chases the suspect, laser-focused on his capture. The ending surprised me as much as it probably surprised you as a reader.

I love to write characters about women and the extraordinary role they play in the world. I love to see women save the day too. In a way, that's what this is about - female heroes that live among us every day and are sometimes called on to do incredible things.

5 We All Must Surrender

The air was crisp and the sky a perfect blue as Alexandra hung the wash on the line. A gentle breeze moved the clothes in waves of fabric. The California air smelled almost sweet, reminding Alexandra of the peaches she'd picked up that morning to make a cobbler.

"Come Ziva, hand me clothes from the basket," Alexandra called to her daughter. Ziva came running.

"Here, Momma," she cried and handed up a shirt. They worked until all the lines were filled with clothes flapping a happy song. Alexandra stretched her aching back, then headed inside their small brick home. Her husband Jacob sat at the table. A pile of bills lay stacked to his right as he worked through their checkbook, balancing it as he did every month.

"How're we lookin', Papa?" Ziva asked, sitting down across from him, a serious air about her as she looked at him.

Jacob reached across the table to ruffle her hair, a smile of pure joy creasing and crinkling his face. "We made a good profit this month."

"Hooray! That means dinner out!" Ziva crowed.

Alexandra watched and smiled at her husband of almost ten years. Ziva had come to them late in life, an unexpected blessing one September day. Jacob winked at her then stood, walked over and twirled her in a small circle. They danced around the kitchen for a moment until Ziva tried to squeeze between them.

"Me next Papa!" Ziva said when she couldn't fit.

Jacob held out an arm for her hand, then resumed dancing, swaying gently while humming a little tune. "My two best girls," he smiled, his brown eyes warm like caramel in the sunlight.

"Can we go early Papa? I'm hungry," Ziva said.

"Sure, Pumpkin, let's get you and Mama ready," he said. Ziva scampered toward the bathroom and Alexandra followed behind. Soon the tub was filling with warm water and strawberry-scented bubbles. Alexandra cocked her head, hearing a strange, roaring sound. It sounded like a train but there were none in the small town where they lived. The hair on the back of her neck raised as the sound grew louder. She moved toward the door. Jacob ran down the hallway toward her.

"Quick, girls, with me!" he cried and grabbed Ziva. Together, they raced for the old basement stairs.

"Jacob, what it is?" She yelled.

"Just come," he yelled back. Jacob slammed the door shut behind them and they moved down the stairs into the dark basement.

"Papa," Ziva wailed, her voice quivering, "I'm scared."

"Shh, Ziva, we're here, and it's going to be fine." Jacob said but his voice quivered. He sat with his back against one brick wall and pulled Ziva onto his lap. Alexandra scooted forward and wrapped herself around them both. The structure groaned, and the roar increased. Water trickled inside from various places.

"Jacob, what is it?"

"It's a tsunami," he replied, looking into her eyes. Seeing the despair, fear, and acceptance there, she clung to them both and tears dripped onto Jacob's arms as the water grew and began to rise. Ziva struggled but Jacob held her close, saying soothing words no one could hear. The roar became deafening. A series of crashes came overhead, and the water increased, rising inexplicably toward the ceiling.

"The water keeps rising, Papa!" Ziva cried.

"We better try for the roof then," Jacob and Alexandra worked to put Ziva on Jacob's back, then half-swam, half-walked through the thigh high water. Above them, the roar had diminished some. Jacob turned the doorknob, then clung to the door as it slammed open, flopping him backward. Water rushed forth, knocking Alexandra from her feet. She was swept backwards off the stairs. She surfaced in the middle of the basement, coughing and sputtering. The water now was to her slender shoulders as she pushed her drenched hair out of her face.

"Alex," Jacob cried, regaining his footing.

"Go on, I'll meet you up there," she said. "Get Ziva to safety."

Jacob shook his head. "Not without you."

"Go, I'll be fine," she said and began swimming toward the door. Jacob hesitated then did as she said. Inside their home, the furniture was ruined but the house had withstood the onslaught of the tsunami somehow. Windows were broken, and the furniture was lined up against the walls like disordered prisoners.

Jacob made his way for the attic, taking down the tiny ladder. He made sure it was firmly planted, then moved up the stairs, testing each rung. He couldn't remember the last time he'd used the ladder, but it didn't appear to have been damaged from the disuse. When they reached the top of the stairs, Ziva climbed down and sat on the floor of the attic. She sneezed and wiped her nose.

"Papa, where's Momma? Is she coming?"

Jacob looked down the stairs behind him. "Alexandra, are you coming?"

There was no response. Jacob looked at Ziva. "I'm sure she's fine, she's probably just having a little trouble getting to the stairs. You watch for her. I'm going to look outside."

Jacob walked over to the small window outside which offered him a narrow view of the neighborhood. As far as he could see was water, several feet deep and flowing very fast. Cars had been swept from their driveways and huddled around trees and houses like little lost children. Several were upside down, electronic turtles stuck on their backs. The devastation made Jacob's heart hurt. How would they get through this? His throat grew tight with grief and fear. How would he keep Alex and Ziva safe?

He swallowed hard several times, trying to loosen his throat. He turned away from the window and went back to Ziva. A roar, like before, began to fill the air. Jacob looked around for something, anything to secure them. A stack of old sheets stood in the corner. He grabbed one, made a knot at each end, then tied one around his waist, then did the same with the other end around Ziva. She clung to him. "Papa!"

"I know honey, just hang on. Hang on to me and the sheet will keep us together, okay?"

He moved them closer to the center of the room and a solid beam there. They waited as the roar grew louder and louder. His heart raced, filling his ears with a drumbeat. "Take a deep breath and hold it Ziva," he yelled and then did the same. The wave hit with a loud crashing sound. The roof was swept away revealing a drenched gray sky. Immediately they were swept up in the current, tossed around like rag dolls, tumbling and helpless through the water. Jacob could feel the weight of Ziva still at the end of the sheet. The water threw them to the surface.

Ziva's head popped up out of the water beside him, her eyes wide with terror. The water moved them forward in a wild current, sweeping them past houses, trees, and buildings of all kinds. Jacob held out of a hand for Ziva and pulled the sheet to bring her closer. She grasped his hand and he pulled her into his arms. He kicked his feet to stay afloat as the current slowed. Ziva clung to him, unable to speak.

They traveled, helpless, as they were carried through unknown neighborhoods. Jacob couldn't tell how far they'd been carried by the ocean waves, saltwater stinging his eyes, only knowing he must surrender to Mother Nature's power if they were to survive. Soon, the water slowed, and a roof appeared with several others on it. With determination, he began swimming toward it with all his strength. One of the men tossed out a rope. Jacob grasped hold. The two men were joined by two others as they pulled Jacob and Ziva onto the roof. Jacob pulled Ziva close. Feeling her shivering limbs made his teeth ache.

"Thank you for your help," Jacob said to the man next to him. "I owe you our lives."

"More than happy to help," the first man replied. Jacob and Ziva followed the man as they made their way to the top of the roof and sat.

"Do you know how high the water is?"

"My home is a two-story and the water's up to the roof-line. About 22 feet, give or take."

Jacob's heart stuttered. "22 feet? Are you sure? Are you in a valley?" Maybe their home was on higher ground. He looked back toward the way they'd traveled. Turbulent water still rushed past.

The man shook his head. "No, we're actually on a small hill."

"Have you seen a woman go by here?"

"Not sure. There's been a lot of things going by but you're the first living thing we've seen."

"Papa, where's Mama?"

Jacob looked around, lost for words. He pulled Ziva closer as she cried against his chest. His heart sank with the realization his wife probably never made it out of the house before the second wave hit.

Author Reflections

This was another prompt-based contest entry. Somehow, all the climate change I've seen over the last thirty years was swirling around in my brain. I've experienced many natural disasters either firsthand (Category 5 hurricane Andrew in West Palm Beach, Florida in the 90's) or from afar (Hurricane Harvey, Houston, Texas, 2017) and this story had to be told. I wanted to make it gripping and personal to the reader. I wanted them to be witnesses firsthand to the devastation - to feel the rush of the water, the powerlessness of being swept along helplessly, so I spent a lot of time perfecting the sensory details as well as setting the stage in the beginning.

But this story is about more than just climate change. It's about surrendering control over life. As humans, it's so easy to believe we're in charge when in reality there are many forces at play that can take that control away in an instant. I've endured that my whole life. It's about the uncertainty of daily life, which is a popular theme in my short fiction. But it's also about family giving us an anchor and restoring us. Finally, it's also about hope for the future. That in all the devastation, there can be a chance for survival and even rebirth.

The name Ziva is an homage to one of my favorite characters, Ziva David from NCIS. I have watched all 19 seasons twice. I loved her character and the musicality of the name so it stuck for the young daughter. The name means "radiance, brilliance, light, brightness, light of God". I found the meaning particularly resonant for the story.

Lastly, this story is to honor the victims of natural disasters around the world. My heart breaks every time I hear about the devastation being suffered by others. In 2021, we endured Winter Storm Uri and went through a week without electricity, water, or cell phone service. It was a horrendous ordeal I hope we never endure again. But as the climate continues to change, I fear this will be yet another part of modern life we need to adapt to and survive.

6 The Oasis

Christine rubbed her temple with one hand and wished the throbbing in her head would end. She tucked her long blond hair behind her ears as she stood and stretched, closing her eyes as the pressure in her shoulders eased. She jumped at a knock at the office door.

“Hey, you okay in here? The door's been closed since you got here and it’s almost two in the afternoon.” Christine’s secretary, Jamie, stepped inside.

“This Donnelly presentation is giving me a headache.” Christine winced and reached up to rub her forehead again.

“Have you eaten today?”

Christine shook her head.

“That's why you've got a headache. Why don’t you go grab a bite?”

"I'll just get something from the vending machine. This presentation will make or break our budget for the next six months. I need to give it all I've got."

"You need a break." Jamie held out Christine's coat and purse. "Go. An hour won't kill you."

Christine rolled her eyes. "Yes, Mother, if you insist."

Jamie laughed. "Just making sure you take care of yourself. After all, you can't give me a raise if you keel over dead."

Christine shook her head as her assistant pulled her to the elevator. Striding into the warm sunshine, she welcomed her midday escape even as she continued to mull over the final touches for her presentation.

Pulled out of her thoughts, she stopped on an unfamiliar street corner. The building exteriors were faded red brick, not the clean granite exteriors of downtown. She looked for a street sign and found none. Crossing the street, she noticed a small restaurant called The Oasis. The rich aroma of spices wafted over her. She stepped inside the dim interior.

A water fountain twinkled and splashed into a shallow pool lit with alternating-colored lights in the entranceway. Lush foliage decorated the interior and created a path deeper inside. Christine followed the plants until they parted and revealed an open dining area. A trellis covered the walls and ceiling allowing ivy to dangle overhead. Shimmering waterfalls cascaded down the walls behind glass panes.

A slender woman in a dark green dress appeared and walked toward Christine.

"Welcome to The Oasis." The woman guided Christine to a nearby table.

"Would you care for some tea?"

Christine nodded, speechless. The restaurant was empty, but she was certain that even if the restaurant were full, it would be just as peaceful as it was now. The woman reappeared and poured Christine a cup of tea.

"Might I recommend our grilled salmon with fresh vegetables?"

"That sounds delightful." Christine wondered how the woman knew what she liked.

"Oh, it's just a knack I have." The woman winked at Christine.

"I'm sorry, what is?"

"Knowing what people like."

Christine stared at the woman. "I'm sorry, I didn't mean to sound rude. I didn't realize I said that."

"You weren't being rude, dear. You didn't say it; everyone asks that at some point or another."

Moments later, her hostess reappeared with a plate and set it before Christine. The salmon was a perfect shade of pink, covered with a garlic butter sauce. Christine took a bite and closed her eyes with pleasure as the delicious flavors flooded her taste buds. She savored each bite, lost in the creamy taste as the pungent garlic and lemon filled her senses. Too soon, the last of the succulent fish and vegetables were finished. The woman returned with a thin piece of chocolate cake. A red strawberry drizzle lay in elegant swirls over the rich dessert.

"I'm sure you saved room for a little dessert? To cleanse your palette?" The woman smiled at her and set the plate before Christine. Christine sliced off a sliver of the cake and knew this was beyond any other meal she'd ever tasted. She ate half the cake before she couldn't take another bite. The hostess reappeared at her elbow as she set the fork down on her plate.

"How was it?" The waitress asked, a knowing smile on her lips.

"Phenomenal. I'd like to thank the cook, if I may."

"I'll be happy to share your appreciation with him. But don't you have somewhere you need to be right now?"

Christine frowned. "Oh, yes, I need to get back to the office and my presentation. But how...?"

"Everyone in this town has places to be. But I am glad you enjoyed our humble meal. I wouldn't worry about your presentation; it'll be great."

Christine stood, gathered her coat and purse, and turned back to face the waitress. The waitress and the restaurant were gone. She stood in a small courtyard with blooming black-eyed Susan's, yellow roses, and white narcissus. A fiberglass garden fountain stood in the center of the courtyard, the cascading water twinkling in the sunshine. Christine turned in a circle, confused.

Was that a dream? She wondered. Goosebumps appeared on her arms. Her headache was gone, her body felt rested and relaxed. Christine looked around the courtyard again then at her watch before she hurried out the gate, knowing exactly what she needed for her presentation.

Author Reflections

This is a prompt-based piece, written in the mid 2000's. Its main theme is restoration and peace within, despite the very fantastical setting. As someone who struggles with migraines regularly and who spent years overworking in corporate settings, I really identified with Christine's situation and the need for both rest and inspiration. This story is a reminder to allow yourself to rejuvenate and relax.

I particularly love the whimsical, fantastical elements mixed with a modern setting as well as all the sensory details from the meal. Sometimes, as a writer, we're transported into the magical worlds we create. This is one of those stories for me. I felt like I could taste every part of the meal, feel the stress easing away.

I'm not sure what inspired this story. It came to me from that magical place where inspiration lives, deep inside.

7

Alone

Her head throbbed in agonizing flashes of pain; the rest of her body ached with exhaustion. Bright beams of sunshine shone through the vertical blinds made her squint to see; lances of pain streaked through her head. Rebecca sat back, legs stretched out before her as her son, Trevor, giggled at a stuffed toy.

"Come on, buddy." Rebecca struggled to her feet and lifted him off the floor. "Time for your morning nap." She groaned as a squeal of protest rent the air. Trevor's wails continued as she walked down the narrow hallway to his room. Lowering the railing, she tucked him in, ignoring the large tear drops that slid down his face.

"Mommy loves you, pumpkin. Sweet dreams." Rebecca muttered, her stomach roiling as she lifted the railing back into place and turned away. Trevor's cries echoed through the small room until she closed the door and rested her back against it, feeling lightheaded. His cries settled into soft whimpers. She grabbed some fresh-washed clothes off her bed and her cell phone, went into the bathroom and turned on the water as hot as she could tolerate.

Shedding her clothes, she stepped into the shower, ready to enjoy a luxurious bath and placed the phone on the floor by the edge of the tub. Steam soon enveloped the room as she rested her head against the still cool tile beside her. She fought against a wave of nausea as her headache increased to an almost unbearable level. She sat down, laid her head back against the edge of the tub and allowed the hot water to pound on her aching body.

Greg pulled into a gas station for a fountain drink and a snack. He reached to shut off the engine just as the radio crackled to life. A tense staccato voice gave details of an emergency call with no response from the caller. He groaned aloud. “Not another false call. That’s the third one this week.” He eyed the convenience store for a moment longer, and then spoke into his mike.

“Dispatch, Unit 242 responding, 3 miles south of location.” Hunger far from forgotten, he slammed the cruiser into reverse and headed north. Within moments he entered a quiet middle-class subdivision of well-maintained homes. He pulled to a stop at the curb. In between two large Cape Cod homes nestled a tidy one-story duplex.

"Dispatch, this is Unit 242 at scene.”

The duplex was a nondescript building, painted dark brown with white shutters. A well-kept garden of pink peonies, bright blue morning glories and brilliant red and orange snapdragons lined the front of the building.

Greg made his way to the first apartment door and knocked. No response. He turned the handle; locked. He knocked once more, harder. He called out in a strong clear voice. "Police, open up." Still no response. A little uneasy, he walked next door to the other apartment and knocked hard.

He heard shuffling at the door followed by the loud clack of a deadbolt being drawn. The door opened in degrees to reveal of rail-thin, gray-haired older woman. "Yes?"

"Good morning, I'm sorry to disturb you, ma'am. We received a 9-1-1 call from this building. Is everything okay here?"

“Everything’s fine, officer. It’s been quiet as a sleeping house cat,” The woman's southern drawl contained a hint of surprise.

"Do you know your next-door neighbor?"

The woman nodded. “That’s Rebecca and her son Trevor. I own the building.” The woman pointed at a beat-up red Subaru parked a little way down the street. “That’s her car but usually she’s gone to work by now.”

Greg frowned. The landlord looked concerned. "Rebecca's sister usually watches Trevor so Rebecca can work during the day but I don't recall seeing her leave this morning."

“I’ll need a key for the apartment please.”

She stepped back and grabbed a set of keys. "I have the master keys to the apartment right here."

"Please stay inside. I'll get these back to you." Greg's heart began to pick up speed, a familiar knot growing in his stomach, as a fresh surge of adrenaline pumped through him. After years on the Chicago police force, his instincts knew all too well not to get worked up over something like this. Maybe she was taking a vacation. Or had been fired from her job. But if that were the case, why didn’t she answer the door? She could be simply sleeping in. The question nagged at him as he took a few steps next door and pounded on the door once more. No response. He inserted the key. The muffled shrieking of a baby reached his ears and his heart rate kicked up a notch.

“Dispatch, entering apartment B. Landlord says the neighbor doesn’t appear to have left for work this morning. There are sounds of a child crying.” His breath came faster as he spoke into the radio on his shoulder and took a few steps into the interior.

"Police, anyone home?" Greg listened hard, gun held in both hands before him as he entered a small foyer. Straight ahead he saw a bright-lit kitchen with spacious counter tops and white cabinets. Greg stepped over a baby gate in the door frame to his right leading to the living room. Colorful baby toys lay scattered throughout the living room. A large television stood in a corner; a sage-green sofa across the room from it. The child’s wailing seemed to reverberate in the small space.

"Police, is anyone here?" He stopped and listened as he surveyed the area. "Can you hear me? Are you hurt?" Silence. Even the child’s cries ceased.

Greg moved through the apartment, and checked the dining room, stepping around scattered toys. His foot kicked a toy and he jumped as the toy's shrill laughter room. He moved toward a narrow-darkened hallway. Greg could hear a shower running. He flung open a closed door to the right. A storage closet. He moved further down the hall to the open door on the right. Gun ready, he peered around the corner and pulled his head back. Sweat began to bead his forehead.

The baby's cries resumed once again. Greg entered the room, his eyes taking in the details. A crib and a short chestnut colored changing table took up a quarter of the space in the room. A wide-eyed toddler in blue pajamas looked at him, his face red and streaked from tears. A strong odor of urine and feces filled the room. A dark, wet stain soaked the front of the boy's clothes. Greg checked the closet; empty.

"Hey, little man. Where's your Mommy?" The boy stared at Greg in silence. "I'll be right back, buddy." Greg turned away, gritting his teeth as the boy began to shriek in an endless wail that reverberated off the walls. Greg threw open another door. It rebounded off a metal rod with a sharp clang. The sound of running water echoed off the tiles. Clothes lay on the floor in a pile. A damp chill hung in the air. He yanked the shower curtain back and felt his heart sink.

"Awww, Jesus!" Ignoring the torrent of icy water cascading from the shower head, he picked up the dark-haired unconscious woman from where she lay crumpled at the bottom of the tub in a heap. A cell phone fell from her limp hand and slid down to rest at the bottom of the tub. Her wet hair dripped cold trickles of water onto his pants and shoes. The narrow bathroom and hallway offered no space to work. He carried the lifeless body out to the living room and felt for a pulse, noticing the blue tinge of her skin and motionless chest.

Keying his shoulder mike, he said, "White female, no pulse, non-responsive. Send an ambulance." Greg began CPR, concentrating on the rhythmic push of his arms, willing her heart to beat as he forced each breathe into her.

“Unit 242, this is dispatch. Ambulance en route. Status update.”

Greg ignored the dispatcher. “Come on, your boy needs you. Come on, damn, you, breathe.” His uniform began to stick to his back and arms as rivulets of sweat flowed down the sides of his face. His breath rasped in his throat as he counted and forced her body to breathe.

Greg lost track of the time, focusing on the steady rhythm of breathing, and pushing, forcing air into the woman’s unresponsive body. The sound of wailing sirens grew steadily louder. A moment later, two EMTs, Mallory and Jake, burst through the door and knelt beside him. Greg found a measure of comfort in Mallory's steady presence. He'd been a part of the EMT force for fifteen years and had proved himself to be capable in high stress situations. Jake, a young, new recruit to the department, had been on two calls so far in his career. His face-tinged red at the sight of the naked woman before them.

"Whatcha got Greg?" Mallory pulled on a pair of latex gloves with practiced experience and felt for a pulse.

"Not sure. Found her in the shower." Greg stood and moved aside to give Mallory room. Two more officers came through the door.

"Hey, we got a weak pulse here." Jake looked up at Greg. "Good job, man. Somebody get that gurney in here." An officer removed the baby gate, and another helped wheel the gurney in as Jake eased an oxygen mask over the woman's face. Together Mallory and Jake worked to maneuver the woman onto the gurney, taking care not to jostle her too much.

"What's going on? Oh my god! Rebecca?" A slender woman, a heavy bag over her shoulder, stood in the doorway. Her face turned a sick, ash white as she stared at the unconscious woman on the gurney then looked up at the officers surrounding the doorway. Her voice shook. "What's going on? Where's Trevor?"

Greg stepped past the other officers and nearer to her. He turned the volume down on his shoulder radio to hear her. "I'm sorry, who are you? "

"I'm… Rebecca's… she's my sister." She continued to stare in horror as the EMTs worked over her sister's prostrate body and strapped her to the gurney. "I'm Cheryl Masters." Behind her, the landlord appeared. Her hand immediately flew to her mouth in horror.

"Can you confirm that ma'am? Do you know this woman?"

The landlord nodded. "That's Rebecca's sister."

Mallory's tense, clipped voice suddenly broke into the crowded room. "We've got defib! Charge the paddles." A pause, then, "Clear!" A loud pop sounded in the room. Greg stepped forward and blocked her view. Cheryl's shock-filled brown eyes, pleading with him to make sense of the chaos, seemed to stare through him.

"Mrs. Masters, I need to see some ID." Greg pulled a small pad and pen from his pocket and guided Cheryl down a hall toward the bedrooms. Another officer stepped toward the landlord and guided her to the door. The EMTs quickly guided the gurney out the door.

"Where's Trevor?" She stopped in the hallway. "I need to make sure Trevor's okay."

"Your nephew is safe. He's in his crib."

"Rebecca was supposed to drop him off this morning before her appointment and when she didn't..." The woman slid down the wall to the floor, muffling a sob with one hand. "She wouldn't answer her cell phone. She carries it with her everywhere. I just figured she overslept."

Greg leaned over her. "Ma'am? Are you all right?"

"Yes." The woman struggled to talk through her tears and rooted around in her purse to pull out a cell phone. "I just... I have to call my husband."

Greg stepped back to give her a little more privacy.

"Jeff, it's me. Rebecca's hurt. No, I don't know what's wrong yet. Listen, meet me at the hospital. The kids will be in school until three, we can deal with them later." Cheryl nodded at the phone. "Yeah, I'm getting Trevor and I'll bring him with me. Can you call Mom and tell her to meet us? Okay, bye."

He reached down to help Cheryl to her feet. Together they made their way down the hall to the boy's room. Two officers stood inside. One held out a stuffed animal toward Trevor, making it dance across the top of the crib rail. Relief lit the boy's face at the sight of Cheryl, and he held out his arms. Babbling gibberish Greg couldn't interpret, the woman swept forward, scooped Trevor up and over to the changing table.

"Cheryl, I know this is difficult, but I need to ask you a few questions, take a statement."

Cheryl nodded and worked efficiently to change the boy and wipe him down, talking in low dulcet tones in response to Greg's questions. Behind him, he heard one of the officers shut the bathroom shower off.

"Does your sister have any medical conditions?"

Cheryl shook her head. "None that I know of. Except for Trevor's birth, she's never been to the hospital. She has been complaining of headaches lately though."

"Do you know anyone who would want to hurt her? An ex-husband or boyfriend perhaps?"

Cheryl paused, stared straight ahead for a long moment then looked at Greg. "No, no one. Everyone loves Rebecca."

"What about the boy's father? Any disputes or custody issues?"

Cheryl shook her head. "No, he disappeared the minute he found out she was pregnant. Didn't want to be tied down."

"Does she do drugs? Been in an accident lately? Acted suspiciously? Have a history of suicide?"

Cheryl shook her head to each question.

Trevor began to scream and flail his little fists in the air. Cheryl jerked around as if struck and began to tuck the diaper around Trevor's bottom. The boy calmed and began to suck on his thumb, reaching for Cheryl's long amber hair with the other hand.

Greg closed his notebook and stepped across the hall into the bathroom as Steve, another officer placed the cell phone in a plastic evidence bag. He spoke in a low whisper as Greg neared him.

"She coded again on the way to the hospital. Looks like she's not going to make it." Together they watched Cheryl as she held Trevor close, talking in a soothing voice to him as she rocked him side to side.

"Too bad it wasn't enough to save her. Pretty smart to carry a cell phone into the shower. I certainly never would have thought to do that." Steve turned sideways to get past Greg in the narrow hallway. "One of the hazards of living alone, I guess."

Greg shook his head. "I saw this all the time in Chicago, and it never ceases to get to me. One day someone's perfectly fine, their whole life ahead of them, and poof! The next day they're dead for no apparent reason."

Greg walked back to Cheryl. "Mrs. Masters, will you be able to take care of your nephew, or do we need to call Social Services?"

Cheryl's eyes filled with tears as she pulled Trevor close. Soft sobs echoed through the room. Trevor leaned back and peered into his aunt's face. "Okay?" One of his tiny hands reached up to rub the woman's cheeks. "Okay."

Cheryl smiled, a smile filled with tears, love, and pain all at once. "That won't be necessary officer. He's always had a home with us. I promised my sister I'd look after him if anything ever happened."

Greg nodded. "Well then, Social Services will be in touch with you once I file my report. Are you alright? Do you need us to call someone for you or anything?"

Cheryl shook her head. "No." She put Trevor down who immediately wobbled toward the hallway. "I just need to gather some things to take to my house."

"Well, if there's anything you need, here's my card. Just call if I can offer any help or if you need a referral for grief counseling. Anything at all, you just call me."

That night, Greg worked long past dark, finishing his report, uninterested in going home to his empty apartment. When the report was finished, he stared at the medical examiner's report for a long time, his eyes unable to leave the words "Preliminary Cause of Death: Brain Aneurysm."

Author Reflections

I wrote this story after almost slipping in the shower one day. At the time, my daughter Libby was only a few months old, I'd recently broken up with my live-in boyfriend, and was completely alone. I was struck by this feeling of intense vulnerability and a vision of what would happen if I had somehow died in the shower. From that, this story was born about the ripple effects even a single death can have on the people around it. It was amazing to me to realize that even for me, there would be an impact on others if I died. It was both humbling and, in a way, reassuring.

On the Edge

It isn't the rush hour traffic or the same daily routine that bothers me. I like routine most days, like knowing what to expect when I get up in the morning. What I hate is every day, trying to come up with the "next big thing", the great idea that will have people sitting up and taking notice. The idea that will cause millions of YouTube hits and viral conversation to span the world on Facebook.

For a marketing executive, the next big thing is like the Great American Novel to a writer. It's the Holy Grail. It's also elusive, like catching dandelion fluff in a breeze. Nowadays, consumers are jaded and fickle, quick to move from the latest gadget to the next amidst a constant storm of competing products and ideas. Few things ever stay relevant long enough to truly be on top for longer than a brief few minutes of glory. Fifteen minutes of fame no longer exists, it's been cut down to about five.

And yet here I sit, trying not to let my gaze become fixed as I listen to Edward, the marketing director, drone on about the latest toothpaste, our next product we've been charged with promoting. Saving America's teeth, one mouth at a time. Could there be any higher calling than this?

"We need something fresh, something new, something no one else has ever done before," he proclaimed, pacing before us and waving his arms with each statement. "I want each of you to get outside the box on this one, be bold."

I looked across the table at Margie, our newest team member. Rumor had it she was stolen from a rival firm by one of the upper management. Stolen or not, she'd shown herself to be quiet, only speaking when she had something worthwhile to say. A cool head in a marketing department can be an invaluable advantage and it didn't hurt she was very easy on the eyes. I watched as a curtain of her long black hair fell forward from behind her ear, obscuring one side of her face as she diligently took notes. I imagined running my hands through those silky strands, her perfect red lips pressed against mine in passion.

Edward clapped loudly, "Great work everyone, let's get to it", and I jerked in my seat, startled from my daydream.

"Wake up time Billy," Andrew, my co-worker for the past three years and cubicle-partner slapped me on the shoulder as he walked past, presumably headed back to our shared office space. I stood to join the rest of my colleagues and return to my desk.

"Bill, can you stay a minute?" Edward said, looking toward me. I nodded and watched as everyone streamed past, headed for the safety and oblivion of their eight-by-ten cubicle villages.

"Go ahead and close the door, would you?"

I complied but stood near it, unsure what to do with myself. I tuck my hands in my pockets, conscious of their sudden dampness.

"So, it's that time of year again, isn't it?" Edward said, looking up at me from where he'd taken a seat at the end of the table.

"Time of year?" I ask.

"Performance review time."

"Oh, yes," I reply, struggling to remember when the actual review was due. I'd received an email about it the week before but only skimmed it. I tried to remember when the actual review was scheduled for and said lamely, "that time of year."

"And, it appears we'll very soon have a senior marketing position opening up. Did you know that?"

I shook my head.

"You've been with the firm for six years now. As the most senior and experienced of the current marketing executives, I would expect you're going to put forth your best effort on this campaign."

I nodded.

"That's good, because I'll certainly be watching." Edward stood. "Oh, and good work on the Donovan Law Firm. The numbers have been really good on that campaign."

"Thank you, sir."

"That'll be all."

I nodded, unsure what else to say and hurried out of the glass enclosed conference room. My mind was reeling. Did that really just happen? Did my boss just tell me I was being considered for a promotion? And if so, did I even actually want it? Sure, it would mean more money but it would also mean longer hours spent hob-knobbing with clients and prospects, plus overseeing a team. But it would take off some of the pressure to come up with new ideas and give me a chance to oversee the idea-generators, a position which had its benefits. Not to mention, senior marketing meant a nice bonus program.

Instead of turning toward my cubicle, I headed toward the break room, sure I'd find Andrew there, hovering around the coffee pot. True to form, there he stood, sipping from his signature coffee cup inscribed with "Carpe Diem: Seize the Day" on it in bright orange letters.

"Hey man, what'd the boss want to see you about?" Andrew asked as soon as he saw me. I looked around the break room, relieved to see we were the only ones.

"A new position's opening up," I said, reaching for a Styrofoam cup. I watched Andrew's face out of the corner of my eye and was pleased to see the surprise flood his face.

"And?"

"And," I said and raised my fingers in a quotation marks sign, "he's going to be watching me. Performance review."

"Dude, that's awesome. Nobody on the team's been around here long enough to possibly compete with you. You're practically a no-brainer for the position."

I nodded, taking in his words.

"We gotta celebrate. Meet me tonight, seven o'clock, at Brady's. First shot's on me."

"You know me; I'll never turn down a free drink." I said, as we walked out of the break room and toward our desks. "But first we gotta come up with something good for this toothpaste." We rounded the corner and on my desk sat a large cardboard box.

Andrew flipped open the box flap and pulled out a square box, "Samples are here." He tossed one to me. The box rattled as I caught it, the toothpaste inside bouncing against the box's confines. I studied the plain packaging before me. It was striped in diagonal green and white lines and labeled "Minty Fresh". Not the most inspiring packaging I'd ever seen.

"What do you think?" Andrew asked.

I shook my head. "I think I could use that shot now."

The bass from the live band made the air outside the bar reverberate and once inside, I feared my teeth might crack from the jarring cymbals and drumbeats. Brady's was a hole-in-the-wall kind of place, with a dark interior perfect for getting close to that special someone and yet tinged with the undertone of stale beer and cigarette smoke. A favorite of college students, it frequently featured local "talent", bands who worked cheap and just wanted an opportunity to get exposure for their music. I looked through the early evening crowd, trying to find Andrew. I made my way toward the bar and spotted him on the other side. He waved to me, and I wound my way through the crowd.

"Hey buddy!" Andrew hollered in between drumbeats. "I hope you don't mind but I invited a few others from the office." I nodded and looked past him. Standing behind him was a dumpy middle-aged man wearing a polo shirt and slacks. Next to him stood a taller, leaner version whose pale complexion screamed computer geek. And standing with her back to the table, elbows propped behind her and waist-length black hair swaying to the beat, was Margie. I felt my chest tighten at the sight of her.

"This is Jack, he's in Accounting." I shook Jack's damp hand and resisted the urge to immediately dry my hand on my pants. "This is Steve from IT." I nodded at him from across the table. "And, of course, you know Margie." Margie turned her head and sent a polite smile my way before returning to watching the band. A Heineken sat sweating at her elbow.

Andrew put both hands to his lips and gave a piercing whistle that could just barely be heard through the reverberating percussion. A waitress in a low cut white top and skin tight black shorts, serving tray in hand, soon appeared. Andrew ordered a round of shots and the drinking began.

After the third round of shots, the band thankfully took a break and some classic rock and roll played through the speakers at a volume a little more conducive to conversation. Jack and Steve began to discuss the processing advantages between the Intel I5 and I7 processors while Andrew flirted with the waitress. Margie stared off into the crowd, occasionally sipping her beer.

At a loss for anything else to talk about, I brought up the only topic I could think of. "So, made any progress on the Minty Fresh project?"

Margie's head swiveled toward me, perfectly arched eyebrows raised above velvet black eyes. "Excuse me?"

"I asked if you've come up with anything for the Minty Fresh project?"

She gave a rueful smile. "Not really. The packaging isn't exactly anything awe-provoking."

"Yeah, I wonder if they got their designer from a Cracker Jack box instead of a proper ad agency."

Margie grinned at me and took a sip of her beer. I felt the silence grow longer and struggled to find another conversation point. "So, how do you like it so far with us at E & M?"

"It's okay. Different from my last firm."

"How so?"

"More collaborative, not so cut-throat."

"Are you from here?"

"No, I just moved here from New York."

I nodded and filed it away in the back of my mind. Being new to the area made it unlikely she had a boyfriend.

"Liking Dallas so far? It must be pretty different from New York."

"Well, it's not the city that never sleeps but yeah, so far I like it."

Suddenly, Margie was shoved hard against the small table in front of us, and her chest bumped into her drink, sending it spinning across the table. I moved sideways as a stream of beer shot across the table. I looked back at Margie, who was shoving a man away, his long dark hair hanging in front of his face. I moved around the table and cupped her elbow, holding my hand against the chest of the man in front of her. A large wet spot soaked the front of her red blouse. The man stumbled around us, headed for the bathroom in unsteady, lurching steps. The smell of beer was suddenly stronger.

"Are you ok?"

Margie nodded and grabbed a napkin from the table and dabbed at her blouse.

"Do you have a change of clothes in your car?" Margie shook her head. "Wanna get out of here?" Margie nodded and after saying our goodbyes, we headed to the door. Outside, the night air had gotten crisp, and the stars shown bright without any clouds to obscure them. I opened the passenger side door to my car, which I'd thankfully parked near the door and when assured Margie was comfortably inside, made my way into the driver's seat. We didn't talk much as she directed me to her place. I pulled up in front of her townhome and hurried around to open her door.

She made her way up the sidewalk, teetering a little on tall stilettos. A crack in the sidewalk almost made her lose her balance and I put my arm around her waist to steady her. She let me brace her as she fumbled to fit her key into the lock. An orange pumpkin stood next to the door, and I wondered if it had been there since the last Halloween. I could tell the drinks were affecting her more than me and hesitated on the porch. She looked at me over her shoulder, "You coming?" I nodded and followed her inside.

"I'll be right back; I'm just going to clean up real quick. Living room is straight ahead, make yourself at home." I listened to her slow steps on the stairs, trying not to imagine her slender legs and the sway of her hips as I made my way down a narrow-tiled hallway and into a spacious living room. A modest flat screen television hung on the wall and a fireplace took up another wall, across from which was a sectional sofa in a deep burgundy. I decided to make myself useful and started a fire in the fireplace.

Margie appeared a few minutes later, barefoot, in jeans and a long sleeve black shirt, carrying two wine glasses half full of red wine. She handed one to me and then sat next to me.

"Andrew told me something interesting today," she said, looking at the swirling wine in her glass.

"Andrew always has something interesting to say," I said with a chuckle. "What'd he come up with this time?"

"I've seen you watching me." She looked at me and I found myself unable to look away. "He says you like me."

I swallowed, trying to think of something to say, unused to a woman being so forward. The complications were too numerous to contemplate, the most cardinal of which is romantic relationships in the workplace. Before I could speak, Margie set her drink on the coffee table in front of us and leaned toward me. Feeling a bit like I was dreaming, I cupped her cheek, marveling at the softness and warmth of her skin as well as her invitation. Her eyes drifted closed, long lashes shadowing her flawless skin. I kissed her slowly, trying to remember to breathe, wanting to savor the rush of heat that blew through me like a lightning bolt. Her lips tasted like red wine and fit mine so well I felt sure I could lose myself in kissing her. I gently cupped the back of her head and ran my fingers through her cool tresses, marveling at the way they flowed through my fingers, like the finest silk, far better than I had imagined. When we finally parted, her porcelain cheeks were flushed with heat, her eyes lidded in drowsy desire. Without a word, she took my hand and led me toward the stairs.

"So, Billy-boy, what'd you do last night?" Andrew asked in a low voice, swiveling toward me with a cocky smile.

I rolled my eyes. "None of your business."

"Did you take her home?"

I didn't respond.

"Well, you're welcome. I knew you'd never make a move on your own."

Before I could respond my phone line rang. Not taking my eyes off the report on my screen, I picked up the phone. "This is Bill."

"Hey, it's Margie."

"Good morning."

"Dinner tonight? My place?"

I nodded. "Sure. What time?"

"Six thirty. Bring dessert if you want."

I said goodbye and hung up. A new window popped up on my screen, a calendar reminder. "Oh shit!" I exclaimed and jumped up out of my seat. I yanked my jacket on over my shirt.

"What's up?'

"My performance review meeting is today. I thought it was next week."

"Good luck, man."

"Thanks," I said, grabbed my notepad and a pen then sprinted down the hall for the elevators.

That night I lay in bed, tossing and turning. The meeting for Minty Fresh was Friday, two days from now and I still hadn't come up with a solid idea to share at the brainstorming session. I looked over at the clock; the bright red letters read two thirty in the morning. My brain was abuzz with images of Margie, the feel of her, the smell of her perfume that still lingered on my skin from our passion earlier that evening. I rolled over, tried to pound the pillow into submission and tried to clear my head enough to sleep.

Just as it was starting to work, I bolted upright, a buzz of inspiration bringing me out of my half-sleep. I scrambled to my desk, brushing aside papers, a broken comb, seeking a pen and paper. I found a pen and yanked a blank piece of paper from the printer tray. In huge letters I wrote "Seize the Day with Minty Fresh!" I stared at what I had written and grinned at the tingle in my fingertips. This would be the idea that would set me apart and secure my promotion into management.

Friday, I arrived early for the staff meeting, print outs of slides as well as a PowerPoint presentation ready to share with the group. I sat in the first seat and waiting, my nerves jangling with the rush of adrenaline from a new idea and the anticipation of sharing it. Everyone began to filter into the conference room at eight. Margie sat across from me with a restrained smile, avoiding holding eye contact for too long. Once everyone was settled,

Edward spoke. "Okay team, what do we have?"

"Edward, I'd like to present a proposal, if I may?" I spoke up. Everyone looked at me in surprise. I knew what they were thinking – it was too early for a proposal.

"Alright Bill, the floor is yours." Edward said and relinquished his seat for mine. I dimmed the lights and turned on the PowerPoint presentation. Dramatic music filled the room as a series of images filled the screen. After a minute, the presentation ended, I turned the lights back up, and sat down to listen to the feedback. For a long time no one spoke.

"I am impressed," Edward said. "That's bold, it's powerful, it's direct."

I nodded.

"Does anyone have anything they'd like to share?"

No one moved.

"Alright, let's put it together. Bill, you'll be lead on this and report directly to me." Once we set up a meeting for that afternoon for everyone to come together and get started putting together marketing materials, designs, and a schedule for launch, we adjourned the meeting.

As I gathered my materials, Edward walked up to me. "That was a really impressive presentation, Bill."

"Thanks," I said.

"You pull this campaign off and I'll be making a direct recommendation for senior management."

I nodded and smiled. "I'd appreciate a recommendation from you sir."

"Keep up the good job."

The spring weeks headed quickly into summer and before I knew it each day was a blur of meetings as we moved into the final stages of the campaign development. One evening, laying on the couch, running my hands through Margie's hair, she looked at me.

"My parents are coming to town next week."

"Okay," I said.

"I'd like you to meet them."

I forced myself to keep my hand steady, to smooth her hair gently down her back, to keep my breathing even and not give away the shock she'd sent through me. After a moment I opened my eyes. "Meet your parents?"

"Yes," she said. "Don't you want to?"

"Well, sure I do. I just wasn't expecting it, that's all," I said. That night, as I headed home, I pondered what it meant. I certainly hadn't dated a lot of women but generally meeting the parents was a pretty serious step and meant a certain level of commitment in a relationship. I wasn't sure an office romance would be looked upon too positively by my boss, especially when being considered for a promotion. I decided to put it out of my mind and just see where things would lead. What harm could there be?

In September, the Seize the Day campaign for Minty Fresh launched nationwide with a series of television commercials and print ads in magazines. A social media campaign rolled out at the same time and the campaign immediately went viral. Never before had a toothpaste commercial been so popular.

A month to the day after the campaign's launch, YouTube registered a million views. Edward brought in champagne, and everyone proceeded to get good and drunk, celebrating the success of a multi-million dollar advertising program.

I stood in the corner of the conference room, listening to Andrew tell another of his many conquest stories, this time about a cheerleader at Texas A & M University.

"I'm telling you what man, those cheerleaders are so flexible. When she would do a split I swear I thought I'd lose it right there."

I took a sip of my champagne and out of the corner of my eye, saw Edward head toward Margie who was refilling her glass. I'd been aching to talk with her all night, wishing the night would hurry up and end. I watched Edward lean toward her and then watched as she threw her head back and laughed at something he said. The feeling of success, so pervasive the whole night, suddenly tasted like ashes in my mouth.

I didn't speak, simply walked in the door.

"Well, hello to you too," Margie said, closing the door behind me.

"What the hell were you doing?"

Margie crossed her arms. "Could you be a bit more specific?"

"With Edward. At the office. Are you sleeping with him too?"

Margie gasped in shock and hurt flooded her eyes. I ignored the guilt that twisted in my gut.

"How dare you!"

"Answer the question. Are you sleeping with him?"

"Of course not," she said. "Do you know me so little that you would even think that?"

"Well, you sure looked cozy enough tonight."

"I think you should leave," Margie said, and held the door open again. "Call me if you come to your senses."

A few weeks later, Edward called me into his office. "Bill, please, have a seat."

I sat in the high-backed leather chair before his office.

"It's come to my attention that you may have engaged in some inappropriate behavior with one of our staff members. Therefore, we've decided it would be best if we brought in an outside candidate to fill the senior management position."

I sat in shock. "What about the Minty Fresh campaign?"

"We'll be putting Mitch in charge of that."

And just like that, just like so many consumer products, replaced by the newest and greatest idea or gadget, so I too had been replaced for the newest idea generator.

I stood, suddenly clear for the first time in what my path needed to be. "Actually Edward, thanks but I'll be submitting my resignation effective immediately." Without a backwards glance, I left his office and headed down the hall to the elevator. Inside, I tried to calm my nerves, hoping against hope I wouldn't be too late. As soon as the elevator doors opened, I headed down the hall and stopped beside Margie's cubicle. She looked up at me, and then sat back in her seat.

"I'm resigning."

Margie raised an eyebrow in surprise but said nothing.

"I was an idiot to you. Worse than an idiot. I was an ass. I don't know what I was thinking. I just hope it's not too late for you to forgive me."

Margie stood and stepped in front of me. "And?"

I stared at her for a moment, at a loss for what she could mean. Then it struck me. This quiet woman, who neither minced words nor used more than was absolutely necessary, had known what I was too blind to see.

"I love you," I said, pulling her into my arms.

Margie simply smiled then kissed me, her beautiful hair falling around me like a silken waterfall.

Author Reflections

This piece is a very early work for me, written somewhere around 2007. It was a time where consumerism became very clear to me as a businesswoman. I found myself disgusted by not only the disposable nature of our purchases but of the disposable nature of our lives. This is the story of one young man finding his way toward an important truth about that. It's also in a small way, about karma.

9

Unbeliever

Her roommate, Amy, lowered her voice to a whisper. “You know what they say, 'On all Hallow’s Eve, the veil between the worlds is thinnest.' Amy sat back and took a sip of her coke. “That’s why there are lights in the graveyard every Halloween. It’s ghosts.”

“Amy, don’t tell me you believe in that superstitious mumbo-jumbo.” Eve snickered and popped a fry into her mouth.

Amy’s boyfriend Brad laughed. “You were born on Halloween, and you don’t believe? Not even a little bit?”

Eve laughed as she reached for the ketchup and knocked over the saltshaker. “Nope.”

“Uh oh Evie, toss some salt over your shoulder or you’ll have bad luck.” Amy smirked.

Eve rolled her eyes. “Halloween is just another day. And there’s no such thing as ghosts. When you die, you stay dead.”

Amy raised an eyebrow. "Prove it. Spend the night in the Cooke Cemetery tomorrow night."

Brad laughed. "I bet she doesn't last an hour."

Eve shook her head. "I have nothing to prove to you."

A deep male voice came from over her shoulder. "What's the matter, baby, scared? I'll go with you, if you want." Her boyfriend Zack grinned down at her.

Eve moved over to make room in the crowded booth full of her college drama friends. *Maybe it wasn't such a bad idea after all.*

Eve smiled at Zack. "Maybe we should investigate. It's probably a bunch of kids horsing around. We could teach them a lesson."

"Alright then, I'll pick you up from your house around dark on Hallow's Eve."

Eve and Zack left the diner at almost midnight to walk back to the dorms. Outside her dorm, Zack pulled her close for a hug.

"Don't go yet," He mumbled into her hair.

She snuggled closer to him. They stood there until his watch began to beep. He leaned down and kissed her, a sweet passionate kiss that filled her with warmth from her head to her toes. When he stopped she looked up at him, dazed. "What was that for?"

"I wanted to be the first person to wish you happy birthday." He smiled. "I love you Eve."

Eve's eyes widened. After a year of dating, they'd never said those words to each other.

"I love you too, Zack," she whispered and kissed him again. They pulled apart and Zack cupped her cheeks in his cool palms. "See you tonight around seven thirty."

Eve struggled to concentrate on her morning lectures. As soon as class finished, she drove to the mall to pick out a new outfit. After several hours of browsing, she found a bright orange top with sequins and a half-sweater that would help her stay warm.

Zack arrived as she finished applying the final touches to her makeup. His eyes followed her every move as she walked downstairs in tight black jeans, sneakers and her new top. Tied back with a black ribbon, her long chestnut hair flowed down her back. His eyes never left her face as he pulled a wrapped present from his pocket and handed it to her. "I got you something."

Eve smiled and pulled the gold wrapping off a long red velvet box. She looked up at Zack. "Zack, what did you do?"

"Open it and find out."

Eve opened the box and gasped. Nestled inside was a delicate filigree gold chain with a pendant in the shape of the letter E.

Zack peered into her face. "Do you like it?"

"Zack, I love it," she whispered. "It's perfect."

"Here, let me help you put it on." Eve turned and lifted her hair for him to fasten it around her neck.

She hugged him tight. "Zack, thank you. This is one of the nicest birthday gifts I've ever gotten."

Zack chuckled. "Better than candy, anyway."

"Definitely!" Eve laughed and put her arm through his as they began to walk toward the cemetery.

"I got it about two weeks ago and it was killing me keeping it a secret."

"I didn't suspect a thing. You're a really good actor Zack."

"Not with you," he said. "You come to my plays, and I almost forget my lines just knowing you're watching."

Eve laughed. "I wish I could give my lines half as good as you."

"Yeah, after the 110th rehearsal, I can do my lines in my sleep." The cemetery gate gave a dry eerie squeak as Zack opened it.

"Where do you think we should go? I can't see a thing."

A click beside her and a bright circle of light appeared on the ground in front of them. "This should help. Amy says the ghosts should be toward the back of the graveyard."

"There's no headstones there though, is there?"

"Maybe we'll see them when they walk by."

Eve shook her head. "How can you believe in that garbage?"

"What, that kids are playing around in the graveyard on Halloween?"

Eve laughed. "I thought you meant ghosts." Eve tripped and fell to her knees.

Zack helped her up. "Hey, you okay?"

"I tripped over a tree root or something. I'm fine."

"Eve, there aren't any trees here."

Eve tried to look at the ground around her. A thin white fog covered her feet. "That's weird. Did you know it would be foggy?"

Zack grasped her hand in his warm one. "Come on, let's keep going."

They weaved between headstones. A cold breeze whipped some of Eve's hair around her face, blocking her vision. With one hand she held it back and followed Zack as he led them through the graveyard. Eve tried not to picture what the decomposed, rotting bodies in the coffins beneath their feet would look like after years buried underground. Goose bumps sprang up on her arms at the thought. Zack stopped and she bumped into him.

"Zack, what's wrong?"

"I thought I heard something," he whispered.

Eve shuddered. "I'm not sure this is a good idea, Zack."

A shrill shrieking came from behind a nearby gravestone. The ground erupted upward in a thick spray of dirt. Eve screamed and clung to Zack.

"Run!" he yelled and began running through the graveyard, pulling her with him. The shrieking intensified as more earth exploded upward. Eve's breath rasped in and out of her chest as she ran.

Eve fell to the ground again. A bony appendage clung to her ankle. Eve screamed and kicked, struggling to break free. "Zack, help me! Something's got my ankle!"

Zack ran back and kicked the bony hand. It released its grip to lie twitching a few inches away. He helped her to her feet. "Come on!"

They ran and Eve tried to ignore the shrieking all around them. They reached the tree line and leaned against a tree, gasping for breath. Eve felt something hit her shoulder and screamed as spiders dropped all over her. Swiping at her hair and clothes, she struggled to brush them off.

The flashlight landed on the ground and cast a long straight light on the ground. Free of the spiders, Eve called for Zack, struggling to see in the darkness. She bent to pick up the flashlight with a trembling hand.

A mottled hand appeared in the light beam, followed by tattered, raggedy clothes. Eve gagged at the radiating stench. She jerked left only to find another creature moving in short, lurching steps toward her. She spun in a circle and found the creatures surrounding her, moaning and shrieking.

The noise stopped, except for the sound of her screaming. She froze at the sudden silence, panting and sweating in fear. Nothing moved.

A bright light appeared above her, blinding her with spotlight intensity. Eve raised a hand to her eyes.

"Happy birthday, Eve!" A chorus of voices shouted from around her. The once shrieking and moaning zombies moved toward her, laughing. Zack walked toward her, grinning.

"You!" She moved to meet him and punched him in the arm. "You did this? You set me up!"

Zack laughed. "Amy thought it would be fun to see what you'd do."

A shambling zombie came up to them and Eve could hear Brad's booming laugh. "You should've seen your face!"

Eve laughed, a mixture of relief and embarrassment. She bent over with her hands on her knees and tried to catch her breath.

The drama teacher walked up and gave her a hug. Eve stared at Mr. Mox. "What? You too?"

He laughed. "Of course! I provided the special effects." He raised a hand, and another spotlight illuminated a large wrought iron fence. Two zombies pulled a black sheet off the fence to reveal two large tables. Someone turned on some Halloween music as Zack handed her a cup.

Zack faced her. "So, what do you think?"

"I could kill you!" Eve growled, glaring at him, then laughed and put her arm around his waist. "That was definitely your best performance yet."

Zack cheered. Monster Mash began to play through the loudspeakers. "Let's party!"

Author Reflections

I am not typically one for Halloween. It's not even a holiday I celebrate. I don't get behind the madness of the costumes and parties, etc. I don't have a ton of close friends and I don't enjoy horror as it gives me nightmares (and I struggle with enough of those on my own). But again, a prompt inspired me despite myself and so I wrote this short piece about a high school prank. It was fun to work on and I hope it gave you a laugh. It's definitely a different twist on Halloween, in my typical personal fashion.

10

A Christmas Proposal

Snow and ice crunched under my feet as I walked up the partly shoveled sidewalk to the two-story brick house of my girlfriend, Bethany's, childhood home. Packages wobbled with each step as I tried to keep them balanced. In my pocket, the corners of a box poked against my leg with each step. Behind me, Beth carried an apple pie and a bottle of red wine.

"Could you grab the door, love?" I asked, craning my neck to look at her. I stepped aside to let her pass.

"Patrick, I told you, you should make two trips. You look ridiculous," she said, laughing at me.

"Yeah, well, I'll look even more ridiculous when they see this ugly sweater you made me wear. I am not sure this is the best first impression to give your family."

"Relax, they'll love you. Trust me," she said and pushed open the door, leaving no room for argument. The smell of apples, cinnamon, and turkey greeted us first. The smell of fresh brewed coffee made my mouth water. Sweet Christmas music played from speakers set up throughout the house. I stepped up the brick steps and over the threshold, holding my breath as the topmost presents hung on the edge of toppling.

"Bethany!" a woman's voice called out. From the corner of my eye, I could see an older, gray-haired woman wrap her in a hug. "You're home! And look at you, you look beautiful!"

"Here, let me help you with that, son," a voice said from in front of me. A couple presents lifted away, revealing a red-faced man who could have doubled for Santa Claus. His cheeks were rosy, whether, from heat or eggnog, I couldn't be sure, A pure white beard hung down to his chest. I wondered if he dyed it that way or if it was natural. He also wore one of the most hideous sweaters I'd ever laid eyes on, covering a robust belly.

"You must be Patrick!" a woman greeted me from behind as more presents were lifted from my tired arms. I realized their wobbling had been from my aching arms trembling. Needed to spend a little more time in the gym.

"That's me," I said, trying not to cringe as she hugged me tight.

"I'm Mirabelle, call me Belle. This is my husband, Carl. Welcome to our home! Can I get you anything?"

"I'd love a cup of that fantastic coffee I smell," I replied, taking in the surroundings. Christmas decorations covered every surface, from the lighted garland on the staircase and fireplace to the sixteen-foot Christmas tree surrounded by a working train set. An ornate Christmas village of hand-painted houses covered various tables. More than a dozen stockings hung from the fireplace mantle, stacked side by side in a row. One of them contained my name in a scrawl of glitter glue.

From upstairs came the sound of pounding footsteps followed by the excited barking of a dog. A whirlwind of colors, limbs, and noise thundered down the stairs. One chocolate colored blur launched itself at me, a small Labrador puppy. I reached down to pet it, but it was gone after the boy who called, "Come on Rudolph, let's go outside!" We followed them into the kitchen where a platter of Christmas cookies surrounded a Keurig.

"Help yourself. Dinner's almost ready!"

"Where's Stacy and Tracy?" Bethany asked, grabbing a cookie as I made a cup of coffee.

"Oh, you know the twins. Running late, of course."

After about thirty minutes of awkward discussion, the twins arrived with their spouses and children, and the meal commenced. A table for twelve was decked out in place settings with a feast fit for a king arranged in the middle. I ate until it hurt to breathe. We moved to the living room to get more comfortable, and I knew the time was upon me.

"Does everyone have a drink?" I asked and rose to my feet with my glass of eggnog. When everyone had agreed, I turned toward Bethany and raised my glass.

"It seems it wasn't long ago when you came in and lit up my life in the most magical ways, from your beautiful smile, to your giving personality, to your amazing intelligence. Having you in my life has changed me forever."

I knelt to one knee and pulled a small box wrapped in gold out of my pocket. From the corner of the room, I heard the mad scratching of claws. I looked as a blur of fur launched itself at my hand and latched on to the box, then took off. Stunned, I looked at Bethany, who looked perplexed. I turned, looking for the thief, who carried the box in its mouth like it had found a great prize.

"Here, Rudolph, here boy," I called and held out my hand, hoping his sharp teeth wouldn't do damage to the package. I crawled toward him on my hands and knees as laughter echoed around me. Rudolph scooted sideways, heading for the door. I dove for him and just managed to grab his hind legs.

"Don't hurt 'im," one of the women called from behind me. I held on as Rudolph released the box to chomp instead on my fingers. I picked him up and handed him to Carl.

"Would you mind hanging on to this for me? He's trying to steal the show," I said. Carl chuckled, winked at me, and accepted the wriggling puppy.

I picked up the box, its paper torn and drooled on. I turned back to Bethany with a sheepish grin. "Sorry about that."

Everyone erupted in laughter, but I only had eyes for my sweet Bethany, whose eyes filled with tears. I kneeled before her, tore off the wrapping, and opened the box to reveal the velvet box inside. All the sound in the room disappeared as I said the words, I'd been dreaming of saying for a month.

"Bethany Stewart, will you marry me?"

Author Reflections

Another prompt-based story that won first prize in a contest. I enjoy flipping around concepts and so this story was born from the idea of Rudolph not being a reindeer but a dog instead. He's a mischievous little rascal and that's why I love him.

11
Life and Truth at a Dinner Party

The inside of the limousine was filled with soft jazz music and dim blue lighting that reflected off the black leather seats.

"Joseph, I'm tired of going to these parties. I don't have anything to celebrate."

"Honey, we've gone over this. This year is more than just a New Year's celebration, it's a celebration of all we've achieved with the cure."

Seraphina snapped, "Yes, we have a cure now, but we couldn't save our son."

Joseph stared out the window.

Seraphina sipped her wine and spoke, "I'm sorry. There's just been so many parties recently. I'm sick of them. I need a break."

Joseph looked at her. "Yes, I know there have been. Everyone's celebrating the ability to gather again. It's a return to the way it was before. Maybe you should take a trip to the Hamptons. Get away for a while."

"Perhaps I'll go visit Mother in Vermont for a few weeks. See the horses on the farm. I haven't been riding in so long. And there's a new foal."

Her husband nodded as the limo slowed to a stop. She studied him in that unguarded moment. He was still handsome after 22 years of marriage. Silver streaked his black hair, but he barely seemed to have aged. She could still see the youth in his face from when they met in college at Vanderbilt University. There were creases around his eyes from laughter. His black Armani tuxedo accentuated his trim build and slender waist, which he kept through rigorous daily runs and rowing. He certainly didn't look fifty years old.

A moment later the door opened, allowing them to exit in front of the historic renaissance-inspired Fairmont Copley Plaza, one of the most luxurious hotels in downtown Boston. Joseph exited then held out a hand to help her from the car. She gathered the bottom of her red satin Stella McCartney gown in one hand and stepped out onto the red carpet in front of the hotel. Soft yellow light illuminated the seven-story building's brick exterior and the street surrounding it.

Joseph paused at the entrance and looked at her. "You look absolutely stunning in that gown." He took in the sheer beauty of her, from her velvety black hair to the teardrop diamonds dangling at her ears, sparkling in the light. His eyes drifted down to her throat where a matching necklace of teardrop diamonds lay at the base of her neck then down to the plunging neckline which displayed her cleavage in an aggressive, feminine way.

Seraphina blushed at his appraisal. It had been a long time since he'd given her his smoky, sultry stare. *Maybe this party wouldn't be so bad after all.*

Joseph turned back to the entrance and led her inside. The soaring ceiling, crystal chandeliers, and ornate blue and gold tiled floors accentuated the expensive red and gold furniture in the lobby. In the back was an unobtrusive check-in desk. A young man in an expensive black suit stood behind the counter and looked up to greet them. "Welcome to the Fairmont Copley. How may I assist you?"

"Yes, I'm Dr. Joseph Connelly and this is my wife Seraphina. We're here for the event in the grand ballroom for Vita et Veritas Pharma."

"Dr. Connelly, Mrs. Connelly - it's such a pleasure to be able to host your event. One moment and a member of our staff will escort you to the ballroom. We'll have staff at the front doors for your guests shortly."

"Not a problem, we're early. I want to make sure everything is set up correctly for the event."

"Of course, sir. Paul will escort you."

A young blonde-haired man in a black suit led them down the hallway to the ballroom. Inside were cocktail tables around the perimeter, with delicate silver-colored chairs surrounding them for seating. The center of the room featured a dance floor. Elegant sparkling crystal chandeliers dangled from the high ceiling. A beautiful painted mural of clouds above gave a feeling of vastness to the room.

In the back was a large banquet table featuring fruit, vegetables, meat, and cheeses, piled in abundance rarely seen in the last decade. Further along were polished stainless-steel chafing dishes with their lids closed. Three sharply dressed waiters stood by to serve. A bar was off to the side with a bartender standing at the ready. Opposite from it was a DJ station with the DJ finalizing his set up. An enormous screen at the back of the room featured the company logo along with a slideshow of images. A soft jazz played from the invisible speakers around the room.

Joseph turned to her, "I'm going to check on the catering, why don't you grab a drink from the bar and greet our guests as they arrive?"

Seraphina nodded and headed for the bar. "I'll take a double vodka on the rocks, with two limes, please." Seraphina took her drink, squeezed the limes into it, stirred it, then took a couple sips. She made her way to the front entrance just as a couple approached, both dressed elegantly. For the next thirty minutes Seraphina greeted the guests, some of which she knew, but there were plenty of new faces. Soon, people had stopped arriving and Joseph moved to the front of the room and stood behind a podium. The logo for the company appeared behind him.

"Welcome to the annual New Year's celebration for Vita et Veritas Pharma. Are you ready to ring in 2030 and the beginning of a brand-new era?"

The room erupted in loud applause and cheers.

"We've spent the last decade working tirelessly on a vaccine to the horrible Covid-19 virus that had threatened not only humanity but the worldwide economy with devastating consequences. Just when the world believed a vaccine wasn't possible, YOU made it happen!"

Explosive applause and cheers filled the room again.

Joseph waited for the applause to die down, looked around the room, then spoke again,

"Millions have perished worldwide. As many of you know, the virus struck close to home for my family, taking our son Jonathan at the age of 20. Life as we all had known it would never be the same. No one's lives were untouched by the virus. But this year, we have brought salvation to the world by taking back humanity's future, untainted by the deadly pandemic. After all these long years, we at Vita et Veritas successfully manufactured enough vaccines for every man, woman, and child. So tonight, we're here to not only welcome the arrival of a new decade, but more importantly, to celebrate all we've achieved for mankind! Yesterday is gone, now is the future, and we saved it."

Loud cheers erupted and the dance music began to play. Joseph made his way off the stage and was immediately surrounded. An older woman approached Seraphina. A white faux fur wrap surrounded her shoulders above a long black dress with double slits at the bottom. Her pale toned legs appeared with each step. Long blonde hair cascaded down her back. Seraphina struggled not to groan. The Vice President's wife, Gina, lived for parties like this.

"Sera dear, how lovely to see you again," Gina said and embraced her, kissing each cheek.

"Gina, how are you?" Seraphina asked, taking a gulp of her drink.

"Doing very well. Are you enjoying the party?"

Seraphina smiled, "Oh you know what they say: "The dying process begins the minute we are born, but it accelerates during dinner parties."

Gina laughed, a shrill peal of laughter that made Seraphina's skin crawl. "That's hilarious, who says that?"

Seraphina shrugged. "It's a quote from a book called 'Among the Porcupines'. I'm sure you'd find it delightful, it's about unnecessary rich socialites."

Gina looked puzzled. "Oh."

Seraphina looked around the room, "I'm sick of being the life of these stupid parties." Seraphina took another drink, emptying her glass. "Pardon me, I'm going to get a refill."

Gina huffed and headed toward another couple nearby. Seraphina made her way toward the back of the room, feeling a little wobbly. The alcohol was doing its good work, soothing her anguished mind. She refilled her glass and sat alone at a secluded table in the back.

Couples danced to the slow song that played and she watched them twirl in their expensive gowns and tuxedos. The wasted wealth surrounding her was overwhelming, making the room feel small and tight around her. She thought of the many children throughout the world starving right now, while these insensible people danced and ate in lavish luxury. She sipped her drink fast, trying to chase away her thoughts. Memories flashed through her mind - the refrigerated trailers serving as portable morgues filled with bodies, the large graves piled high with the dead. Her son, in the ICU, failed by the machines around him, as she held his hand, willing him to live and take another breath. Her son's face as he lay in his casket, so still and lifeless.

Seraphina whispered to herself, as a tear escaped down her cheek. "I wish it had been me. It's all my fault. I'm sorry I failed you son." She finished her drink and stood, her legs trembling a little. She stumbled toward the front of the room, trying not to trip over the chairs. She needed air and to get away from the stifling room and her haunting thoughts. She made her way to the elevators and pressed the button for the top level to the roof.

The elevator bell dinged, and the doors opened. In her intoxicated state, the sharp frigid December air had no effect. She stepped forward and looked upon the Boston skyline, a nearby church steeple's spire piercing the night sky. She walked to the railing and tried to peer over it to the ground below. The tall black bar kept her back from the edge. The urge to see below grew and she saw a nearby wicker couch. She walked over to it and kicked off her heels. She climbed up onto the ledge, shaking just a bit. She slowly stood, looking toward the horizon, studying the lights of the city. Then she looked down toward the ground. Cars rushed by on the street below, their lights bright, fast-moving spheres in the darkness.

She wondered what it would be like to jump. Would it feel, briefly, like flying? Would she finally be free from her consuming grief and anger, if only for a moment? The urge was tempting, even though she had no desire to die. She slowly spread her arms out, closed her eyes, and just stood still, gently buffeted by the winds. She embraced the adrenaline and exhilaration coursing through her body. She considered the duality of it all: standing, full of life, on the precipice of death, and being in control of both domains at once. She was their master.

"Seraphina, what the hell are you doing?" Her husband shouted from behind her.

She jumped, startled, and turned, one foot finding only emptiness. He screamed her name, his desperation and terror resounding through the night as he raced toward her. Her mouth opened in a wide O as she crossed the boundary into emptiness and their eyes met.

For a short eternity, it felt like falling in nothingness, surrounded by complete silence. She stared up at the wispy clouds filling the moonlit sky, her soul and body finally free.

Author Reflections

Of the entire collection, this story might be the one I like the most. Written about six months or so after the lockdown for COVID-19 began, I tried to envision what the future could look like in a post-pandemic world. I tried to create a lot of contrasts between the haves and have-nots as well, something that was very apparent to me at the time as I read stories of the rich fleeing to islands and isolated compounds in panic.

At the time of this writing, we're only 1.5 years into the pandemic but lives are changing every day from it. It's far from over unfortunately. This story is about my hope that one day we will find a way to end this pandemic for good and the world can move forward and heal. There will be loss and pain, but those that remain will hopefully still have a bright future.

12 Seeking Redemption

My sister stood on the doorstep, suitcase in hand. Since our family reunion last year, she had changed her pink spiky hair to a midnight black. It hung disheveled and tangled down to her shoulders. Black makeup caked her lips and ringed her eyes. Wafer-thin and pale, she looked like a hungry dog left out in the rain.

I moved aside and watched as she stepped across the threshold. Closing the door, I turned to face her. "What are you doing here, Bea?"

She stood for a long moment and the silence grew larger. It crept into all the nooks and crannies of my tiny apartment, an almost visible presence. "I'm sorry." She wet her lips and looked at the floor. "I didn't know where else to go."

I noticed my apartment now contained a new smell; dank, musty, like the contents of a closet in an abandoned hundred-year-old house. Her dirty black clothes hung off her as though they'd been draped over a wire hanger.

"What happened to you?" I asked.

Beatrice sighed, a shuddering exhale full of sorrow and defeat. "A lot."

Seeing the sadness in her face, I realized how little she resembled the carefree younger sister I used to know. What happened to the pig-tailed girl who ran up to me after school, eager to share stories about our day?

I smiled gently at Bea as I took the suitcase from her. One hand on her shoulder, I guided her toward the bathroom. "Why don't you take a hot shower? I have some clothes you can wear. Then we'll get some lunch, I know this great deli a few blocks from here." Bea nodded and disappeared into the bathroom.

I gathered some clothes out of my closet, a pair of comfortable jeans, a loose t-shirt and a fresh towel. I laid them on the counter in the bathroom and returned to the couch. I turned on the television for background noise but found myself unable to concentrate. Faces flashed across the screen. I gnawed at my fingernails.

Thoughts bombarded me. What the hell's she gotten into now? How am I going to tell Mom? So, help me, if she keeps me from my date with Jeff, I'm gonna kill her. She has no right to barge into my life like this. Bea emerged from the bathroom towel drying her hair, pink splotches on her cheeks from the shower's heat. Her pale face, scrubbed clean of makeup, looked innocent and fresh.

"Thanks, it's been a long time since I had a good shower."

I jumped up, nervous and needing to do something, anything, with my hands. "You ready?"

Bea nodded and returned the towel to the bathroom. I grabbed my keys and a pair of sunglasses while she slipped into a pair of my sandals. A light breeze kept the warm summer air comfortable as we walked for a block without saying a word.

I spoke first, looking straight ahead. "You look tired."

She walked beside me, watching the sidewalk pass under her feet. Bea's eyes met mine and for the first time, I saw the pain and anguish within her. At 24, she had seen and done horrors I didn't want to imagine. She nodded and looked back at the ground. "I've had a rough year."

I felt a pang of guilt. I had no idea what had happened in her life since I'd seen her last. Bea and I were inseparable as children. Our mother did the best she could, raising us by herself, but she had little time or patience for two hyperactive girls who wanted nothing more than to climb trees and terrorize the neighborhood boys. Somehow, Bea always managed to cause more mischief; from early on, trouble seemed drawn to her.

"Do you wanna talk about it? Are you in trouble?"

Bea laughed, the sound hoarse and bitter, coming from deep inside her chest. "Not any more than usual."

We arrived at the door to the deli, and I forced myself to hold onto the anger simmering in my chest. We found a corner table away from some of the other patrons. Once our waitress had taken our drink requests, Bea spoke first as she shredded a napkin into tiny pieces.

"I'm just tired of my life being so hard, you know Diana?" She looked up at me. "I'm tired of having to do it all alone, having to struggle so hard every day."

Bitterness rose deep within me. As if it has been easier for me? I swallowed hard, choking it down.

The waitress interrupted us with two glasses of ice water. Bea proceeded to gulp down her drink. I slid my glass forward for her once she had finished.

"I'm tired of the drugs, the sex, all of it." Bea took a breath. "I wanna stop. I want my life back."

I stared at her, unsure of what to say. My voice came out cracked and crumbling, like a dry riverbed. "What do you want me to do about it?"

"Can you help me?" Her royal blue eyes looked at me, pleading, tear-filled.

I inhaled a deep breath, and remembered telling her the year before she needed to slow down. The memory of her words ripped me open and this time the anger overflowed.

"'You don't know anything about anything', isn't that what you said to me?" I gritted my teeth. "You made your choice long ago, remember? Why should I believe you now?"

Tears spilled down her cheeks. "Oh God, I'm so sorry. You're my sister - I never should have said that."

I looked away for a moment, watching some of the other patrons enjoying their lunch. "I don't know, Bea. You can't just expect me to pretend it never happened."

"I know." Bea leaned toward me. "I'll do whatever it takes. I'd just like a second chance, an opportunity to make it up to you."

The waitress returned with our food. I took a big bite of my sandwich, trying to think of a response. Bea's food sat before her, untouched.

"Aren't you going to eat?"

"I don't know." Bea leaned back against the chair. "I don't feel so good."

I frowned at her. "You drank that water like you were never going to see any again. Probably gave yourself a stomachache."

"Actually, I…" I watched horrified, sandwich halfway to my mouth, as my sister collapsed to the floor.

I dropped my sandwich. "Bea! Oh my god, someone call 9-1-1." I threw myself to my knees beside her and pushed Bea onto her back to feel for a pulse.

The next few moments passed in a blur. A group gathered around us and I heard their whispers to each other, asking what had happened. I vaguely heard a woman talking on a cell phone giving an address.

I held Bea's hand. Time lost its hold on my senses as I prayed for the ambulance to get here. The seconds seemed like multiple eternities as I rocked beside her, tears spilling unchecked down my cheeks. The ambulance pulled up to the door, siren blaring and lights flashing.

Paramedics rushed in, efficient and steady in their actions and questions. I backed up until I bumped into a chair and fell into it. A woman knelt in front of me, and I realized she had on a paramedic uniform.

"Ma'am?" The woman looked concerned as she peered into my face. "Ma'am, can you hear me?"

I nodded. Her questions buzzed through my mind like a chainsaw cutting trees. Did Bea take any medications? Did she have any prior medical conditions? Prior hospitalizations?

I answered each question like a shattered war hero, unable to focus on anything but the sight of my sister as the paramedics worked to roll her onto a gurney. I leapt to my feet when they began to wheel the gurney to the ambulance. I climbed in behind the technicians and focused on holding her cold hand in mine, watching her chest rise and fall with each breath, willing her to stay with me.

At the hospital, I answered more questions, filled out forms, and then began to pace in the sterile waiting room. Three other people sat in the room, staring at a television hanging overhead broadcasting the day's woes to a vacant-eyed viewing public. I checked the clock, then turned to walk to the nurse's station to demand an update. I bumped into the nurse behind me.

"Miss Summers?"

I nodded.

"Your sister's conscious. You can see her now." I followed the nurse down the hall to a semi-private room with two beds. Bea lay in a bed at the farthest end of the room. I moved into the chair beside the bed and grasped her hand. Bea's eyes fluttered open, and she turned her head to look at me.

My throat clogged with emotion, and it took me a couple tries to speak. "Hey, Bumblebee, how you feeling?"

Bea gave me a weak smile. "You haven't called me that in ages, Di." She paused. "But I feel like shit, thanks."

I chuckled and wiped away tears of relief. A large man entered the room, dark red hair adding a morbid splash of color to the plain white of his coat and the bright white walls. I thought of blood and forced myself to look away.

"I'm Dr. Carter." He looked down at the chart in his hand then back at my sister. "Beatrice, our blood tests show extremely elevated ketones and blood glucose. Do you have a history of diabetes?"

I stared at him in shock. "No, of course she doesn't. No one in our family has ever been diagnosed with diabetes."

"Certainly, a family history could be an indicator but doesn't preclude a possibility of diabetes existing."

Beatrice averted her eyes. "I was diagnosed three weeks ago."

My mouth dropped open in shock.

The doctor nodded and scribbled a note. "Have you been taking your insulin?"

Beatrice shook her head.

"May I ask why?"

"Well, I know what the doctor said but I thought if I quit all the drugs, I wouldn't need insulin anymore."

A long pause filled the room before the doctor spoke again. "Beatrice, you don't seem to realize the seriousness of the situation. You've done permanent damage to your body. Diabetes doesn't just go away. What you've suffered from today is called diabetic ketoacidosis. This occurs when there's too little insulin in your body for an extended time frame. It causes your body to break down fat for energy instead and releases toxic acids known as ketones. Have you had any nausea, vomiting, abdominal pain, fatigue, anything like that?" Beatrice nodded to each one.

"You need to take better care of yourself in the future, Beatrice. That includes taking insulin daily. I'm going to recommend you stay here for observation a minimum of two days. We've got your IV in so we'll start with plenty of fluids and electrolytes through the IV and a regimen of insulin. If you've improved by then, I'll send you home with diet instructions and an insulin regimen. You'll need to see your regular physician for follow up care within three days. Understood?"

Beatrice nodded, looking at her hands twisted in her lap.

I stood up. "Doctor, she's going to be okay, right?"

"That's up to her. If your sister takes care of herself, she'll be fine." He smiled at me and turned to leave. "I'll see you again in the morning, Beatrice. Try to get some rest, your body could use it."

I watched him pull the curtain back around us before I turned back toward Bea.

Bea's eyes closed tight.

I sighed, feeling an enormous weight of grief and guilt weigh down on me. "Bumblebee, why didn't you tell me? Why didn't you call me?"

Bea opened her eyes, and I could see the tears in her eyes. "Di, I was such a wreck – all strung out from the detox. There were nights when I begged for drugs, anything to take away the agony. Most of the time I didn't even know my own name. I couldn't let you see me like that. When I got out of the hospital, I felt okay. I didn't see any reason to upset you."

I laughed. "Oh sure, this is a much better way to find out."

Bea gave me a tired smile. "Yeah, I see that."

I pulled the chair closer to the bed and tried to put the emotions from the last few hours into words. "Bea, look, it doesn't matter what happened before. If you want my help, you have it. All you have to do is ask. Always. I'm sorry I made you feel like you couldn't come to me."

A sob burst forth from Bea's lips. "I'm so sorry, sorry for all of it. I'm sorry for letting you down, for not listening to you sooner, for hurting you."

Tears formed wet rivers down my cheeks. I leaned forward to hug her as she wept against my shoulder. When her sobs had slowed, I sat back and handed her a tissue from a nearby box.

"You need to rest. I'm gonna go home and grab a few things," I gave her a quick smile, "since we're going to be vacationing at the University of Chicago Medical Center for a couple days. I'll be back in a few hours, okay?"

Beatrice smiled as she nodded, then leaned her head back and closed her eyes as a nurse began to set up a new IV bag. I watched for a moment and then turned to find my way back to the car. A forgotten place within me felt full again.

Author Reflections

This might be one of my favorite stories. It came at a time when I was reconciling with my half-sister and was born from the question of how do you bring together two people who have drifted so far apart? Sadly, while this story has a happy reconciliation with hope for the future, my own was much messier and ended once again with estrangement. But this story is still a testament to the power of forgiveness and love, which is what I love most about it.

This story is published in *the Drastic Measures anthology* (available on Amazon) alongside the venerable George Clayton Johnson (*Ocean's Eleven, Twilight, Star Trek*). It was one of my earlier short stories to be published and I was delighted to be published alongside such experienced authors. I was also interviewed by a news station in Irving, Texas for both this story and my children's book which was published a couple years later.

13 Gone Nuts

The rhythmic slap of her sneakers on concrete set a steady cadence to her pace. Each controlled inhaled and exhaled breath kept her focused on putting one aching leg in front of the other. The early morning sunshine flickered through the trees as she ran, feeling her heart pound in her ears.

Every morning, Elizabeth jogged the same path; a half-mile to the park, four complete laps of the one-mile jogging trail, and then a half-mile run back home. Often, she would pass pets and their owners out for morning exercise and the occasional cyclist. They would exchange the customary nod and continue along their chosen path.

Today, however, she happened to come across an older man walking a long-legged German shepherd. She tried not to laugh as the dog, panting and choking with excitement, dragged his owner along.

"Slow down, Rudy." The man kept one hand on his brimmed hat, and another on the leash. "The grass will still be there."

She jumped to the side as the dog dragged his helpless owner into her. "Hey, watch out!"

Turning sideways to avoid colliding with the man, she wound up tangled in the leash instead as they stopped. The canine's brown-eyed gaze met hers and for a moment, she thought the animal was laughing at her.

"I'm so sorry." He wiped sweat from his forehead. "He's a little excited today. Are you okay?

"Yes," Elizabeth said, unwinding the leash from around her legs, trying not to sound impatient. "Fine."

"Nice legs."

"Excuse me?" Elizabeth stared, her mouth hanging open.

"What?" He looked at her, puzzled. "I didn't say anything."

Elizabeth looked but could see no one else around. Her eyes narrowed and she backed away to continue down the path.

"Hey, I'm talkin' to you."

Elizabeth jumped. The man's mouth hadn't moved. He continued to stare. "Sure you're alright, miss?"

"Did you hear that?" She looked around again. He shook his head and began to look at her with concern.

"Wow, you're hot, but you're dumber than a poodle. Down here, blondie, the German shepherd."

Elizabeth froze, unwilling to believe her ears. She looked down at the dog facing her, tongue lolling.

"Hi there, gorgeous. The name's Rudolph, but you can call me Stud."

Elizabeth took a step backward. "You've got to be kidding me!"

"Does this look like the face of a dog who would kid you?"

"But," she took a deep breath, "how is it you can talk?"

"Just lucky I guess. I can read too."

"You mean street signs?"

"Sure, books and magazines too. I just love a good Playboy, they have the best articles. I'm trying to learn French right now. A cute little French poodle's teaching me. Wanna learn some French?"

“Sorry, I have to get going.” She edged away from the animal and his owner, watching them the whole time.

The man stretched a hand out to touch her. "Miss, what’s wrong?"

She turned and sprinted away.

“Can I get your number? Hey, where you going?” The dog shouted as Elizabeth began to put distance between them, running full speed along the trail. Thirty minutes later she arrived at her front doorstep, drenched in sweat, her breathing hard and erratic.

“I must have gotten a bad flu shot.” Elizabeth shook her head as she fumbled to fit her key into the lock. "Or else I need my head checked. ‘Cause I’m losing it."

A loud noise made her shriek and drop her keys. She turned her head to look behind her. A squirrel sat a few feet away, sniffing in her direction, paws outstretched.

“Got nuts?” the squirrel asked in a high-pitched voice.

Elizabeth giggled and said, “No, but I’m pretty sure I’ve gone nuts.” She reached a trembling hand down for her keys. The key slid home. She opened and closed the door then leaned her back against it. Elizabeth closed her eyes, and wiped the sweat from her face, trying to catch her breath.

A soft female voice interrupted the silence. "What took you so long, young lady? I've had to pee for ages."

Elizabeth screamed and stared down at her shitzu, Missy. Her pet looked up, brown eyes peering through the white fur surrounding them. "Well, don't just stand there. Let's go,” Missy said, then walked toward her leash and tugged it from the wall as Elizabeth fainted, her body crumpling to the floor.

Author Reflections

I wanted to end the fiction section on a lighter, sillier note. This piece resonates with some people and not with others. I always intended it to be a very straightforward story. A woman goes out for a run like any other day and begins to hallucinate. The why isn't important. Sometimes in life, the why isn't the point, it's the experience.

PART TWO

Nonfiction

14 Writing From My Soul

If someone had told me twenty years ago, when I first read The Black Stallion, I would be forever hooked by written words, I would have never believed I would be here. Years ago, as a young child, my father abused and molested me. My mother abandoned me at 10. I was in pain and fear constantly. Books saved my life. They transported me into fairy tales, far away places, new unexplored worlds. They gave me horses so that I could ride away from my life, fast and free as the wind.

It would be almost twenty years before I realized the depth of my love for words. I learned it wasn't just reading them that I loved. I loved shaping and arranging them, lovingly placing them in a way that would transport my readers somewhere magical. Even then, I didn't imagine I might want to do or be able to do for readers what authors had been doing for me. At fourteen I wrote my first short story for an English class. I discovered a new kind of magic - even more powerful than reading books. I fell hopelessly in love with writing.

As I grew, I used words to heal myself. I wrote about my pain, my fear, and my hatred of the world. I wrote about betrayal, sorrow, and joy. I wrote about my circumstances and how they affected me, how I would change them if I could. I wrote my hopes and dreams and my journey to fulfill them. I poured it all out and over the years, it kept me sane as I remained trapped in a repeated cycle of victimization and abuse. It kept me from losing the small, fragile part of me that remained hidden away, where no one could find it.

Once I became an adult, I realized a new freedom: the freedom to choose my own path. As soon as I could, I freed myself from my abusive prison. I fled my life and determined I would start anew, unaware that demons still followed me and threatened my new life at every turn. With each success, it seemed I found an even bigger failure. But I continued to read and write through the years.

My writing became a form of self-therapy. I used writing to heal myself, to soothe my soul. The magic of words rid me of my pain, battled my demons, and then created new magical worlds for others to play and be free in.

I write now so that never again will my voice be silenced. It will rise; pure, clear, and beautiful, to touch all who will listen. It will whisper secrets, share dreams, protect and love. It will live on through the ages, and find those small children and adults who are like I have been, and are holding onto a pain that they should release. It will find others and share beauty and joy and pain and fear. One day, my words may save someone else, as words have always saved me.

Author Reflections

I wrote this for an exercise that asked why I write. The truth is I write because I must. The stories build up in me and must burst onto the page. And after 25 years, I doubt that will ever change. But it's also one of the hardest things I do. Creating vibrant worlds, characters, and images doesn't come easily. Every word takes effort. Writing is love and dedication.

I have a vision of readers in my mind: curled up in a chair under a warm yellow light, reading into the late hours or curled up in bed under a cozy blanket. It's my hope these stories transport you, that they engross you and envelope you. Lastly, I hope my writing is something you revisit over and over and share with those people who matter to you in life.

15 Lost

There's a dark, soothing place within my mind that no one knows about. No one else may enter without my permission. The doors are sealed by magic, the entranceway is hidden and once there, I don't leave until I'm ready. I seek refuge here and stay for long periods of time, the durations growing longer each time. I just sit in the darkness, soothed and calm, uncaring of anything except for the peace and safety.

Outside me, the world rages. Pain racks my physical body and senses as blows strike me, but I stay safe in my secret place, lost to it all. No one can touch me here, I've made certain of that throughout the years, increasing the magic, strengthening the barriers to keep others away.

Then the day comes when the raging stops. My body has healed from its wounds, but I stay hidden, fearing a trick. A year passes, then two, then five and ten. Slowly, I dare to step free from my secretest of hiding places. I stand outside the door, trembling in fear.

The meadow that I once tended with love and care is gone. In its place are weeds and dead trees. Where birds once sang, now silence reigns. I walk and I walk, but I'm lost, unable to find my way. I grow weary, my will begins to fade, and I sit for a long time, unafraid but so tired I don't know how I'll ever stand again.

A voice cries out in the stillness, "You're free! Just be free!"

I leap to my feet and look all around. "Who's there? Can you help me? Please, I'm so lost. Please, please, help me."

"Come to me, I'll help you."

I begin to run now, as fast as my feet will carry me. I leap over the dead trees and weeds, fast as the wind. "Please, don't leave. I need you." And I run faster still. It seems like ages, running, running toward the sound of that sweet voice until I reach a beautiful valley. The trees have new buds on them, just starting to bloom like in spring. The new flowers dance in the breeze and a group of horses graze off in the distance.

A figure appears off to my right and I stand still, knowing somehow this is who I seek. She draws nearer and I begin to laugh. I rush forward and embrace the shining, beautiful woman before me - for she is me and I'm no longer a lost little girl, but a woman set free.

Author Reflections

I spent more than a decade doing therapy off and on to deal with childhood trauma. As part of that healing process, I had this dream and decided to turn it into a short fiction piece. It is a moment when I learned for the first time that I could love myself. Original draft was written in July 2008 when my daughter was six months old.

For me, true change and a search for peace began with the birth of my daughter. As she grew, day by day, so did I in ways I never expected. I continued my cognitive behavioral therapy, two hours per session, twice a week. It took more than two years of hard work on myself and this piece was part of that process.

16

Shadows of Darkness

My dreams are never actual dreams. They are always the same – a soothing white fog. Endless walking, aimless and unhurried. It is so peaceful. I want to stay there forever. The shock of the alarm clock or my father's voice would rouse me each day to instant wakefulness, fearful of his anger. Another day of pain would begin.

When my sleep is disturbed this time, however, it isn't to the early gray of morning. The room is blanketed in the shadows of darkness. Invisible hands brush against me, pulling and tugging at my clothes. I lay still and squeeze my eyes shut. My heart beats in my chest so hard I can hear it in my ears. I struggle to breathe slow and even, feigning sleep.

Who are you? What do you want? What's happening? Where am I? Don't touch me! Just leave me alone!

The hands begin to tug harder, trying to pull me over onto my back. I allow myself to remain limp, letting my body flop uselessly. The hands become insistent, pulling harder. Tears burn behind my closed eyes as my clothes are moved aside. Clammy hands touch my bare skin. I whimper and scoot away toward the edge of the bed.

No! I'm asleep… I'm asleep… I'm asleep. Don't touch me. Oh God, please, don't touch me again.

"Shhh.." an unrecognizable whisper drifts through the shadows of darkness. "I won't hurt you."

Icicles of fear stab my insides and I begin to tremble. I move to the edge of the bed and stand.

If I can just get away. Please, let me get away.

Keeping my eyes closed tight, I move around the end of the bed and hurry into the bathroom. I close the door and turn on the light. The mirror reflects my pale complexion, bright green eyes wide and staring. Alternating black and white tiles reflect in the mirror's vision. I reach behind me and push the locking mechanism on the door, slow so it won't click. I sink down against the cool tile, bare legs on the floor. Soon I curl up on the floor, tears leaking from my eyes as I stare at the tile.

I doze off and on, dreamless until I jerk awake a few minutes later, heart racing, goose bumps of fear across my arms. The doorknob rattles and I scoot away toward the toilet. It turns once, twice, three times, caught short by the lock. Minutes pass with no sounds. Hours later, shivering from having lain on the cold tile for so long, I open the bathroom door, peering out. The bed sheets are crumpled in a heap at the foot of the empty king-sized bed.

Did I dream it? Was it all a dream? Please let it have been a nightmare.

I move to the window and draw aside the curtains. Bright sunshine greets my tired eyes. For now, the shadows of darkness are banished.

Author Reflections

This short piece took more than 20 years to finally write and is based on a real life dream I have been having much of my life. Calling a dream isn't right really - it's a memory and it haunts my dreams. It wasn't until I met my husband, Robert, that I felt the courage to seek a place to publish it. I was honored and humbled when Awakenings magazine not only published it but later, asked for an audio reading to promote it.

In July 2021, I learned my father died from COVID-19 in January 2021 and it was one of the most ecstatic moments of my life. The monster who had tormented me for 25 years and beyond, was finally gone. I do not hate easily. He was the one and only person I ever fully hated, and it wasn't until I had my own daughter that I learned how much I hated him. As a parent, one of my worst nightmares has always been about someone hurting my daughter as I was hurt and so I worked hard to prevent it.

His abuse took so much from me - innocence, confidence, fearlessness. He robbed me of something precious and irreplaceable. Despite that, I found a way forward. I found strength and courage and fierceness within me that might not have been possible without all the many struggles that came before.

I have worked hard my entire life. My father told me I wouldn't amount to anything, and I would never be a writer. I've spent three decades proving that lie wrong. Other people have made me feel ugly and small and worthless but two men, Skip and my husband Robert, stepped forward and make me realize that as long as I love myself, no one can ever take that away from me.

I've been blessed to find love and support around the world, even as others choose to walk away. This story was one of my first and most important steps toward all of that.

17

Metamorphosis into Mom

As a single woman in my mid-twenties, I never envied my friends with their domestic lives and young children. The idea of becoming a soccer mom was revolting to me. I sneered at mini-vans. I was absorbed by my career, my hobbies, and my writing. I adored my freedom to come and go as I pleased and was content to keep it that way. I had no interest in and could see no reason to get married. I had no desire for kids, or so I told myself.

In the summer of 2006, however, I found myself staring at the word 'pregnant' on a home pregnancy test. The realization my life would never be the same hit me so hard I couldn't think. I couldn't breathe.

When I remembered to breathe again, I realized I was excited and scared about this unknown adventure. Everything in my life lacked purpose, a direction. Each day was the same as the one before. I pushed thoughts of diapers and midnight feedings and temper tantrums out of my head. For better or for worse, I was responsible for this life. I would make the best of it. I became a single mother and I refused to look back.

I wish I could say I made immediate changes in my life or I had an epiphany about how I should live. It was and continues to be a daily metamorphosis. In the first few months, the only things that changed were my gynecologist got more frequent visits from me than before and I began to throw up more than I ever have in my life.

I did not have an easy pregnancy. By the second trimester and after testing every prenatal vitamin on the market, we realized the vitamins made me ill. My only choices were to take anti-nausea pills throughout my pregnancy or stop the vitamins. There were more risks with the anti-nausea pills, which were actually for cancer patients. I decided to make sure my growing baby received all the nutrients she needed through my diet with minimal supplements. I ate Flintstones vitamins daily like they were candy. I chose the latter option believing women had been able to have babies for years without modern medicine. With my doctor's help, I learned what it would take to ensure my baby got everything she needed. My pregnancy progressed well and on February 28, 2007, my healthy 7 lb 11 oz daughter was born by cesarean section.

Everything I had done to prepare for her arrival, everything I'd expected, paled in comparison with the reality. I had dreamed of her, both awake and asleep. I'd imagined how she would look and chose a name for her I hoped would suit her even though I'd never seen her face. Her baby clothes were neatly arranged in her room and waited for her to wear them. But when her blue eyes met mine, I was transformed. I was filled with an indescribable love I'd never experienced. I became a mother. Everything until then was practice for this moment.

I didn't think or hesitate. I jumped into motherhood with both feet. I refused to allow the nurses to put her in the nursery at night, preferring to take care of her myself rather than be unable to sleep without her. It took four days of patience and effort before she was able to breastfeed without help from at least one nurse. I celebrated every time she nursed, proud we had navigated that important task with minimal effort. On day five, we headed home, confident and comfortable with each other.

In the first month, I learned more about myself than I thought possible. I learned to be coherent and lucid on three hours of sleep. I became adept at changing a diaper with my eyes closed. I learned everything I had believed about babies was untrue and the reality was better than anything I ever imagined.

From the start, I celebrated her every milestone with unabashed enthusiasm. My best friend, whom I admire for her effortless ability to mother four children, became my shoulder to lean on and my guide when I have an issue I can’t resolve. If my daughter wouldn’t sleep, or wouldn’t stop crying, I called her. Together we celebrated my daughter's first smile, first tooth, and first laugh.

Now, I celebrate not only my daughter’s milestones but also my own. Every day is a new challenge to understand, nurture, teach, and care for this tiny person who changes every day it seems, while also juggling a full-time career. I’ve adapted, evolved, and developed, as if by magic, into this new person known as 'Mama'. I’m proud of what I’ve become, especially when each night before I lay my daughter in her bed, she rests her little head on my shoulder and hugs me goodnight.

Author Reflections

This was one of my first nonfiction pieces to be published and helped me to realize my nonfiction career would become an enduring part of my life for decades. It was published in 2010 in a small regional paper as part of a column about motherhood.

18

A Mother's Love

There is something so cruel about life. It took you from me, at only 13. Earlier, really. Oh, you're still alive, in a way. Your eyes are still the brilliant blue I love, like a perfect Texas sky without clouds in spring or like the perfect bluebonnets you love so much when they bloom everywhere. You still smile, creasing your cheeks, but inside your mind is twisted and darkness consumes you. I couldn't see that for so long. All I see, even now, is my baby girl. Who I carried inside me for nine months and played with you through my stomach as you grew. Took care of you in the first days and months as they became years. When you were afraid of grass, I grew confused along with you. How could grass possibly hurt you? But in your three-year-old voice, all you could tell me was it would eat you. Little did I know then how much the darkness would grow to consume you. So, you avoided the grass. And I did too. It became normal to us both. You were so perfect in my eyes and soul, so happy, I couldn't see it - the beginning of the darkness.

I can't blame you for the darkness inside you. You come by it naturally, even though countless doctors in their pristine white coats, will never understand what I know. The darkness that lives in both families, mine and your father's. My father, who molested and tortured me my whole life. He tried to consume me, tried to twist me, tried to inject his darkness into me to destroy my light. He failed. And there are times I wish he hadn't. If he'd killed me all those years ago, I wouldn't have to live with this pain, this grief, this horrible, soul-sucking despair that overtakes me if I think about you too long. But then I wouldn't know the joy either -- that lives inside of me too.

Your first words: Pretty Mama. How it lifted my soul to the heavens as you patted my face and smiled and said those sweet words, just for me. Pretty Baby. Pretty Libby. Pretty Mama. I took joy in teaching you new words: ball, dog, kitty. I delighted in your first shaky steps, your pudgy little legs struggling as you tried to figure out how to make your legs move. Watching you grow, teaching you about the world became my life's mission. I would be better for you and through that *betterness,* I would make the world good for you, through my sheer willpower. Instead of the darkness I have known all my life, I would surround you and protect you with light and love - I would inject my light into you.

I didn't know how strong the darkness could be - how even my light could only do so much, despite my desperation to overcome. How I would give anything to absorb it from you, to take on the burden of the horrible hallucinations that haunted you all day. I would have gladly taken it all - the voices that drove you mad all day with their incessant whispering, poisoning your mind against yourself. And with each new medication, I had hope as I saw the darkness pushed backward. I couldn't know or predict how brief it would last nor how it would roar back with such force. I couldn't imagine how your mind would shatter, like a million kaleidoscopes. When they said schizophrenia, when they said bipolar disorder, I foolishly had hope. Finally, we had a name for the darkness—surely that meant they could fix it.

Finding a seven-inch butcher knife under my bed stopped me cold. For the first time in my life, I lost. I lost huge. I lost the most important things I'd ever been entrusted with—your love. Your sanity. You told me in great detail how you would murder and mutilate me. At first, I was horrified to believe I was the person all your darkness was aimed toward. How could that be? But then you described how you wanted to kill anything - that they were going to die anyway, so why shouldn't you be able to indulge in your dark visions of murder and death? I realized my love—a mother's love -- would never be enough to combat this darkness. Nothing can. It is a battle only you can fight.

But no matter what the outcome, I send my love out into the universe—hoping somehow—it can still save you.

Author Reflections

This is a deeply personal piece for me. I wrote it when I was devastated and despairing over my daughter's mental illness. In 2020, things got as absolutely bad as they could get. Our family hit rock bottom and I was forced, against my will, to accept the reality I had lost my daughter to the mental illness inside of her. At the same time, I learned the truest depths of unconditional love.

Despite my daughter detailing in full detail to me how she wanted to murder and mutilate me and our entire family, I still loved her as much if not more, than I ever had. It proved to me, unequivocally, there is nothing she can ever do that will change my love for her. I wrote this piece to address the grief and the love, twin forces that exist within me so powerfully they defy words.

I also still, despite it all, have hope one day she will find healing and peace, even if it's not through me. I now understand how mothers can still love their children after the child has committed terrible atrocities. A mother's love is special and can never be destroyed. I will love her until the day I die and beyond.

It also just goes to show you can survive far more than you think you can. I thought the grief would be my undoing and if I'm honest, it was close. It was scary. But somehow, I reached deeper into that place within me where there is strength and resolve and courage and found a way forward. I leaned on my husband, my friends, and my family. I made it through the darkness to the light once again.

19 Liberty

To this day, I remember writing the words, "I don't care if you die. You're already dead to me." My rage burned, absolute and fierce, within me. I meant every word. My therapist said I needed to write a letter to my mother but never send it. I ignored the last part. What did I care about the relationship? My heart held no reconciliation for her. I suffered through so much hardship, struggling to find myself a path in life without the support of any family. I blamed her. I felt so alone. More than anyone, she should have been there for me. My rage lashed at her. Was it right? Was I punishing her? I laid out my pain and suffering at my father's hands in brutal, explicit, graphic detail. I used every ounce of my writing skill to slash at her, eager to wound her, desperate to hurt her with every word.

I was twenty years old when I sent it, ten years after my mother left in the middle of a perfect spring day. I had returned home, happy and excited from elementary school, ready to tell her about my day. She was gone, leaving the house an empty, silent shell. No note. Empty spaces where her things had been. No explanation. It felt like a sucker punch to the gut and I couldn't imagine what I'd done to make her leave. As children do, I blamed myself. I wasn't a good enough girl, even though I wanted to be. And I missed her so much it hurt to breath.

I didn't know it then, but that moment changed my life forever. For four years, my mother didn't call or write. I had no idea where she'd gone or if she was dead. No longer having her as a protective buffer allowed my father to abuse me in every way possible. He tormented and molested me for the next four years. Then my mother came unexpectedly back into my life and offered for me to come live with her. I jumped at the chance, anything to get away from my father. Little did I know how messed up my mind was from the abuse at my father's hands.

My mother tried to give me all manner of freedoms, but I didn't know how to act. I struggled academically, socially, and at home. One of my friends tried to commit suicide. I made friends with just about anyone, which included a young Latino gang banger in the neighborhood. He would walk me home from school and ask me if I wanted to hang out. I never let him in. One day, he invited me to his house to meet his mother and in the dark empty house, raped me on the living room floor just inside the door.

I fled home, terrified, in pain, confused, and ashamed. I ran away from home, unable to face my mother, to an abandoned house near a school friend who brought me food and water for three days. I made plans to kill myself with a razor blade. I cut off all my hair. A neighbor reported kids going into the house and the cops showed up to return me home. My mom, unaware of any of these details, had enough after nine months of my behavior and sent me back to my father. A few months after I moved back in with him, he went to jail for selling drugs. Finally safe from him, I spilled my story to a social worker. I was put into foster care the same day.

Adding insult to injury, when social services finally located her, she refused to accept me back in her home. She told them I was out of control, a liar, and a slut, having sex with any boy willing. I suffered new abuses in an insufficient, overwhelmed system. After escaping it and my father's influence, I spent over a decade battling impossible demons. I loathed myself. I believed I was unlovable. My father was unforgivable, but my mother, to me, was responsible for it all. If she hadn't left me, life would be different. Someone would have loved me, and it would have all been bearable.

Life taught me to be humble, giving me numerous lessons. At 26, I learned I was pregnant. My world changed. My unstable life wasn't suitable for motherhood. I began therapy twice a week. I promised to be a better person for her and fought to fulfill my promise. I named her Liberty, hoping it would serve as a talisman against abuse, tragedy, and the horrible circumstances filling my life.

Her birth filled me with an indescribable love. I became obsessed with being a good mom. I read books, took parenting classes, and reached deep within myself for new strength. I discovered compassion, empathy, and understanding for the world around me. The raging beast within me quieted.

Soon, I realized some important truths. Being a mother is hard. The decisions we make, the love we give, the balance we walk, is a fine line. Doubts came. Maybe my mom never knew a monster would come for me when she left. How could she? Would I have somehow known? Was I expecting her to have a crystal ball into the future?

When Liberty's father abandoned us and disappeared, I was devastated for us both. While I found deeper understanding, we faced homelessness before Liberty's second birthday. I had to choose: take her with me or leave her behind.

It's amazing how cycles, choices, and history repeat. I agonized far longer than I ever believed I would. Why was it such a hard choice? Did my mother wrestle with doubt before leaving me? I always swore I would never leave my child behind. But faced with reality, I was torn between protecting her and keeping her close. The idea was tempting to leave her with someone else.

"Just for a little while, until I get on my feet again," I told myself. But would I follow in my mother's footsteps almost two decades later? My best friend with four kids offered to take Liberty and would keep her safe and fed. Would I lose my child in the process?

The time came to choose, and my daughter chose for me. She cried, screamed, and in her tiny, perfect voice said, "Don't go, Mommy! Don't leave me!" I thought of my mother, who left during a school day, unable to face me, knowing I would do the same. My heart, once rock-like and burning in its self-righteous anger, softened toward her like warmed butter.

A mother's job is hard. It's 365 days of the year for the rest of your life. It's not a job, although it is work. It requires selfless devotion of the mind, heart, and soul, committing to another human being, saying, "I'll always be there. You'll always have a place in my heart." My choice was made as if there were no question at all.

I realized then not all of us are capable of such devotion. At times I thought I wasn't. I reached deeper and found a way. I took Liberty in my arms, turned my back on safety and security, and forged forward. We spent our first night in a privately-run women's shelter. Sleepless, I sang nonsense to her under my breath and held her close as she slept in a cavernous room with bunk beds lining the walls, surrounded by six other mothers and their children. It was the longest night of my life. I wept, fearful of the future. Had my mother done the same her first night alone?

The next day, we found another shelter. A week passed, bouncing from shelter to shelter, terrified of disease, physical attacks, and being robbed. I considered sleeping in my car. Then I found a local program run by a group of Christians who offered long-term housing and help recovering from homelessness for women with children and no criminal or drug history. We'd found a place to spring from.

I set to work. With their resources, after a year and a half, we moved from Indiana to Texas, ending our homelessness for good. Against my will, I began to understand the choices my mother faced. Did I find strength and understanding because of my experiences and her leaving me? I chose to believe she did what she thought best at the time. I realized resources and solutions were more limited in 1989 than they were for me in 2005.

I know now, I'm not my mother, even though I'm influenced by her still. I also know when faced with impossible situations, how hard it can be to choose, and to do the right thing. I forgive her. While we don't have a very close relationship today because of being in two different states, I am at peace with it all. And Liberty set me free.

Author Reflections

It's amazing how much things can change with time and new perspectives. It's been 21 years since I wrote the letter to my mother. Finding the ability to forgive my mother was something I struggled with almost my entire life and it wasn't until 2019 I was able to do so. It took a combination of education and life experiences to give me the ability to understand the life circumstances that led to her decisions. Sometimes, that's just how life works. I'm much less quick to jump to decisions as a result.

Forgiving her was incredibly freeing. Giving her grace allowed us to have something of a relationship. It's true time heals all wounds and 31 years later, that's at least one wound that's simply a scar now. I will never know what life would have been like with her in my life during my teenage years but the experience made me stronger. And it also made it so I didn't make the same mistake myself.

What I now know about trauma, after a decade of therapy, has helped me to understand not only my life, but my parents' lives and our family history. Abuse and trauma really are cycles that repeat. I was fortunate to have motivation to break those cycles in myself and our family so hopefully it breaks the pattern for our children and the next generations.

20 Nani

I wasn't looking for a dog. Before I became a single mother to my daughter, I was a die-hard cat person. Cats adored me. Or so I thought. For Thanksgiving 2010, my fiancé Ryan and I drove with our kids to visit his best friend Robert at his home in Bastrop, Texas. It was just a quick visit of a few hours. Robert, his wife Angela and their kids lived on an acre of land off a road that was lucky to be called a road. It was a 65 mile per hour fear fest, and I was driving. We missed the driveway twice.

When we got out of the vehicle we were greeted by a cacophony of barking, followed by what was a multicolored blur attacking the gate. There was a small sea of animals milling about so fast the only distinction that was clear was colors. Fortunately, they quickly grew bored with us and moved away when the door to the house opened.

We were escorted past the noise into the relative quiet of a sprawling single story ranch style house. A couple of dogs milled around inside in a much more leisurely pace and there was thankfully no barking.

One dog, a heavily pregnant female strolled toward me, ears forward, intelligent brown eyes fixed upwards on my face as if demanding I make eye contact with her. Her face radiated welcome and kindness. I knelt down to let her sniff my hand. She brushed past my arm and immediately snuggled up against me, toppling me onto my rear on the hardwood.

I chuckled in surprise at her forward nature as she nuzzled my hand for petting. Her fur was pure silk and softness to the touch and very dense. I was astounded further when this dog I had just met made herself at home in my lap, all thirty pounds of her. I have always been good with animals, but this was something else entirely. My fiancé and his friend emerged from the kitchen, and both stopped in their tracks. Robert's jaw dropped open.

"Well, I will be damned!"

I looked up at him, continuing to stroke the dog's fur. "What?"

"I've never seen her take to a perfect stranger like that. Shelties are normally skittish and shy around strangers, especially her. Her name is Nani, which means Mother. "

I grinned up him. "I think I might be in love." I looked at my fiancé, but his face was empty of expression, not a good sign.

Robert's wife came out of a hallway in time to hear my comment. "Really? We plan to retire her soon and need to find a home for her."

"You're kidding?" Without a thought I said, "I'll take her." My fiancé's shock was completely ignored by everyone, but I noticed.

I looked down at Nani and she met my graze without hesitation, then nuzzled my hand for more rubs. I was smitten and the deal was struck. In exchange for one final breeding and first pick of the litter the next heat, she came home with us.

The first year was a real adjustment for us both. She had been raised from birth as a breeding dog and had been 100% outdoors her whole life. Carpet confused her and our small apartment with its many noises of neighbors, police sirens, and car alarms confused her even more. We discovered quickly that loud noise would cause her to howl in fear and perfect unison until it stopped. She didn't know the first thing about dog toys or what to do with them. She gorged herself at every opportunity and quickly gained five pounds. Then ten. With no dogs to fight over food and plenty of it, she had a feast every day. But the one thing she learned fast was that she could sleep beside my bed every night. Because of her heavy coat she didn't cuddle or lay in bed, but it wasn't unusual for her muzzle to find my hand in the middle of the night and nuzzle it. I am not sure who she was reassuring, herself or me, that she was she there and we were together. I think we both thought it was a dream come true.

She loved me completely, fiercely, and without hesitation. Her days were leisurely, and since I worked from home, we spent all of our time together. She seemed to live for the walks we took. I taught her how to walk on a leash, which she took to with little hesitation, never yanking against it like other dogs but would gently keep step with me no matter the speed I chose. We played fetch and she would bark herself into a frenzy. She took to fetch with a natural, exuberant relish, as if she'd been waiting to do it all her life. I taught her tug of war and we would tug the rope between us around the room growling playfully at each other, oblivious to everyone else.

It was a relationship unlike any I had ever experienced. Her love was unending and her loyalty without question. I was her person. She shied away from all others without my encouragement and a reassuring rubbing.

The years passed for us both. I got married, then quickly divorced, we moved numerous times, kids got older and around the time I noticed my own first gray hair, Nani's hips started to bother her. Our walks and games grew fewer and shorter. She began to hop downstairs until finally she would fall up or down them. Her spirit was so strong and completely determined to be with me. Her eyes were still clear and bright, but her fur began to degrade. It lost its luster and began to fall out in clumps. Our vet said she would keep going long past the time she should for sheer love of me, but a time would come when she would be unable to eat, or sleep. We knew her time with us was ending.

Many nights I sat on the floor and just held her and cried while she licked my hand or face. Six years was too short to lose my best friend. Our family worked to say goodbye and I struggled to find strength to let her go. I wrestled and agonized over it for weeks until we finally decided to do it after the new year. Then she went 72 hours without eating or sleeping. She was in so much physical pain she just laid flat on the floor and panted or paced endlessly. She could find no comfort in anything.

We decided it was time and instead of waiting we called the vet. We found a caring local vet to help us put her to sleep and brought her to him. I sat on the floor and held her like I always did. I told her over and over how much I loved her as they gave her pain medication and tranquilizers to relax her. After an hour she started showing some signs of relaxation but no signs of sleep. They gave her more tranquilizer with no visible effect. We played some pretty music for her in tribute then gave the vet the go ahead. I held her head as she gave a sharp yelp and went limp. I kissed her one last time and fled from the room, desperate to escape her sightless eyes that always looked at me with such love.

I rescued her from a loveless existence, but she rescued me into a complete one. Her love completely changed my life. It's been eight months since her passing, and it still hurts just as much today as the day I said goodbye. I cherish the memories of her, and I would not hesitate to rescue her again if given the chance. I didn't even know I needed her, but from the day we met, we rescued each other every day.

Author Reflections

It's hard to believe it's been six years since I wrote this piece. I still miss Nani. Losing her wasn't the first time I'd lost a pet, but it was the first time I'd ever put one down before. Somehow the guilt ate at me for a long time. I know it was the right thing to do. She deserved a peaceful end to her suffering but how I wish I'd had more time with her. Forever wouldn't have been enough.

Isn't it amazing how these beautiful creatures come into our lives and completely change them forever? Nani's love and our special time together is still something I treasure within my heart and soul. I'm forever grateful she picked me, and I had the opportunity to have her in my life. Since her, we've had Max for seven years and he's starting to show his age now. He is a heart worm survivor, so we expect his lifespan may be short too. We'll be grateful to get a few more years with him but his hips are going bad. A few years after Nani, there was Precious, a black cat, who died unexpectedly at 3 a.m. one Christmas and was buried in our front yard in Temple. Then there was Rory in 2021, who has brought such a bright energy to our home. She loves to prance and dance around. When I leave, she perches at the nearest window and doesn't leave until I come home.

The animals we bring into our lives are a gift to be treasured. The grief over losing them never disappears, it just becomes more manageable. This piece still makes me cry to this day.

21 Stop the World

I am here today for one reason: someone stopped me.

The house was vacant and abandoned in a neighborhood a few miles from my house. I had been there for three days, hiding from my life. In it, I found a discarded razor blade in the bathroom. I held it in my hand and then used it to shave all the hair from my forearms. The sight of myself in the mirror disgusted me. Grabbing a handful of my shoulder-length hair and using the razor, I cut it off. Clump after clump fell from my hands as I shaved my bangs off to my scalp. I screamed myself hoarse. Thick strands littered the dirty floor around my feet.

Crying and shaking so much I couldn't stand, I sat in the closet. I didn't deserve sunlight or warmth or space. I was dirty, a monster. I was a bad girl and no one in the whole world wanted me or even cared. No one was looking for me. It would be better for everyone if I wasn't here anymore. I should kill myself. Then it wouldn't hurt anymore. My father hated me, beat me, and touched me in ways that confused me and made me sick to my stomach. My mother couldn't stand me and screamed at me constantly. She blamed me for her life. I had no friends - the only one I'd had, killed herself. What was the point in living? It hurt to breathe.

I held the razor against my wrist, ready to cut. But how? I didn't know. Then I heard a sound. I froze, afraid to breathe. The window in the room opened, metal screeching against metal. Was it going to happen again? Was someone here to kill me?

I scooched into the corner and hid. A walkie-talkie squawked gibberish. Keys jangled, and a voice rang out in the house. "Hey, I know you're in here. This is Officer Spalding. Someone heard you screaming." His voice sounded warm and calm, not angry. "I just want to help you. You're not in trouble. I promise."

I bit my lip and closed my hand around the razor. I would use it if he was lying. "I'm in the closet," I said and crawled toward the opening. I peeked out and saw him standing in the center of the room, arms at his sides. I noticed he had blue eyes. He smiled at me.

For a moment, I smiled back.

"Why don't you come on out and let's talk for a minute?" Then he sat on the dirty gray carpet and crossed his legs. He said something I didn't understand into the radio on his shoulder. I crawled forward and sat next to him. I crossed my legs and put my hands in my lap, razor still hidden in my right hand.

"What's your name?' he asked after a moment.

"Charity," I said.

"Do you have a last name?"

I gave it to him.

"How old are you?"

"14."

A long silence filled the room. I could hear birds chirping outside.

"So, why are you in here all alone?"

I shrugged and picked at the carpet.

"You look like you might be sad." He shifted, trying to get comfortable. He leaned forward to rest his arms on his knees.

I nodded.

"Okay, do you want to talk about it?"

To this day, I still don't know why, but I trusted him. His eyes were clear and friendly, and he just looked nice. His voice was soothing and calmed me. Before I knew what was happening, the last three days came tumbling out.

I told him about the neighborhood boy who I thought was my friend. Who I thought liked me. Who held my hand, sending shocks through my arm. Whose smile lit up my insides in a new way. How he wanted me to meet his mom. He brought me in his house, where there were no lights and all the windows were closed. Then he pushed me to the floor, took off my clothes and forced his penis inside of me.

I wept as I recalled the pain, the fear, the smell of his sweat, the sound of him above me. How I screamed and kicked and begged and then just fell silent as he finished. Office Spalding then did the most amazing thing. Very slowly, he put his arms around me and held me as I sobbed. He waited while I caught my breath. I told him how I came to the house.

"So, what happened to your hair?"

"I cut it."

"Oh? What did you cut it with, scissors?" He looked around, then at me.

I shook my head, then held out my hand and opened it. "With this."

He took a deep breath, "I see. Can I have that?"

I nodded, and he plucked it carefully from my hand. He tucked it in one of his many pockets. With his arm around me, we talked. I told him everything.

"You are one brave, beautiful little girl. None of this is your fault. Sometimes in life bad things happen, and we must find a way to work through them. Killing yourself isn't the answer. You are precious, and you are so important."

"You think so?"

"I know so. Now, I'd like you to make me a promise. And this is a solemn vow you can never break. Do you think you can do that?"

I nodded.

"You're going to go through tough times in life. You'll want to give up and believe you're better off dead. But I want you to promise me you will never take your own life. I want your word you won't ever kill yourself."

I sat for a moment, thinking about what he said. I looked at him, and something from within me spoke. "Okay, I promise."

"Thank you. That means the world to me. Thank you for trusting me. Now, what do you say we get you back home? I'm sure your mom is really worried about you."

I hung my head. "No, she's not. She doesn't care about me. I doubt she even called anyone to look for me. She's gonna be really mad."

"She might be mad. Running away from home is serious and something you need to not do again either. I'll talk to your mom, okay?"

I nodded, and he helped me to my feet. We climbed out the window and walked out to his squad car. There was a crowd gathered around, strange faces I didn't recognize. Three police cars, blue and red lights flashing, formed a semi-circle around the driveway to the house. He opened the front door and I slid into the seat.

I don't remember much of what we talked about on my way home, school, things I liked to do, but mostly I was quiet. I was tired. I was still scared. I thought of my promise and wondered how I could live up to it. My mom was livid, but not because she was worried. She couldn't believe I'd been brought home by a cop. She never even reported me missing. A few weeks later she sent me back to live with my dad.

Twenty-five years later, I still remember Officer Spalding's words. They're sealed within my soul in a special place I use in case of emergencies. He was right. There have been many hard times since. Times I thought I would have to break my promise. But something just won't let me give up, no matter how much it hurts. And his words ignite the part of me that refuses to quit. He was my guardian angel. He saved my life.

I have used the same strategy with my own family – my daughter, who struggles with mental illness daily, my son, my husband, friends, colleagues, clients, and myself. I have honored that promise every day since and I always will. I have saved four people so far. I hope to keep saving more.

As it turns out, I am important. I just didn't know how much until many years later. Now I am important to countless people, but mostly to three special, wonderful people who I love beyond words. I carry his message with me and share it with all who need to hear it. Because if I'm important, you are too.

Author Reflections

This is another piece that took a long time to emerge. It won "Best Essay" and a $1,000 prize in 2019. In life there are people who come into it and are brief flames while others are longer-lasting. Detective Spalding was an incredibly brief flame, but he changed my life forever. I will never forget his kindness and how it healed me. This story is to honor him and the many officers around the country who sacrifice and care for others, especially now in a landscape where it is more dangerous than ever to be in law enforcement. He is my hero.

I share this story as often as possible because I know there are people in the world every day who are filled with despair, who have lost hope, and are thinking they cannot go on. I've been there. I've been there a lot. I struggle with constant depression as a result of childhood trauma. I'm here to tell you: you can go on. You simply must make the other choice, the choice to fight. Your life matters. YOU matter. YOU are important. And if you give it enough time, you'll come to realize it too. So, keep fighting and never give up. I promise if you do it long enough, things will change for the better. I spent almost my entire life struggling - through pain, darkness, poverty, and trauma. If I can survive all of that and find the other side of things, the happier things in life, I promise you can too. So don't give up.

If you don't feel like you're strong enough to do it alone, there are resources. You can call the National Suicide Helpline at 800-273-8255 in the US, 24 hours a day, 7 days a week. There are a lot of options if you search for suicide help, which includes chat and text if you're not comfortable talking to someone directly right now. I hope you choose to live, like I did. It was the best thing I ever did.

I admit it regularly surprises me how much this story has resonated with people. I receive messages all the time. Every year, I celebrate suicide prevention month in September and every year in December, as part of my birthday I collect donations for the National Suicide Helpline. I've learned little things can make a huge difference. Search for me on Facebook and you can join in the donation drives.

About the Author

Award-winning author Charity Marie loves dragons, wizards, and swords. She also loves writing and reading stories of all kinds. She's a certified Paralegal and a former Realtor. She lives in San Antonio, Texas with her dogs, Rory and Max, her teenage son, and one incredible, patient husband. She is an avid professional poker player and a passable cook. She also enjoys coloring and painting. She hopes one day to have a successful vegetable container garden.

Visit her at http://charitymarie.com

or connect with her on Facebook, Twitter, or LinkedIn

for information about upcoming releases and more.

More from Charity Marie

Other Available Books

Jason, Lizzy, and the Snowman Village

Jason, Lizzy, and the Ice Dragon

Pending Releases (2021)

How to Adopt a Dragon

Jason, Lizzy, and the Luckless Leprechauns

Future Releases (2022 and beyond)

Jason, Lizzy, and the Dark Fairies

Cherry Blossom Tree (a novella)

Most Wanted: A Jazz Macintosh novel (Book 1)

Angel Deveron Trilogy

Hometown Homicides: A True Crime Series

www.ingramcontent.com/pod-product-compliance
Lightning Source LLC
Chambersburg PA
CBHW081135300726
48982CB00005B/973

* 9 7 8 1 7 3 7 8 8 5 4 0 5 *